Suzanne,
To Drinking [illegible]
Job! Great Aussie
Wine & Beef!

I DRINK on the JOB

A REFRESHING PERSPECTIVE ON WINE

Charlie Adler

ISBN: 1-4392-6869-X
ISBN-13: 9781439268698

CONTENTS:

PREFACE

When I first set out to write this book, I began creating an introduction to a wine book that would attempt to cover all the bases. The goal was to cover the major wine topics, such as the world's great wine regions, secrets to food and wine pairing, health and wine, etc. When I began planning the format of the book, I realized I was making the same mistake that many writers in the past have made—attempting to "simplify" wine. After over a year of putting my thoughts to paper, I realized that it's simply impossible to explain wine on paper, and even worse, it's really dull to read about!

I Drink On the Job is not meant to be the one book you can go to for all the answers to every potential question you may have about wine—plenty of those kinds of books already exist in the market today. Instead, this book is the culmination of teaching and attending the most popular wine class in the history of Washington, DC: TasteDC's *Wine Basics 101* class. With over sixteen thousand attendees in just over a decade, this introductory wine class is by far and away the most influential beginner's wine class in the DC area, if not in the whole Mid-Atlantic. More people in our area have learned to sip, schlurp, and swallow a variety of wines from TasteDC's efforts—from wine tastings to cooking classes to embassy functions—than any other similar classes I know of. I've learned more about wine and the people in the wine industry from simply organizing and attending my own events than I could have if I had spent the same time in a wine store or working as a sommelier in a restaurant.

I've probably heard every imaginable question about wine, and it amazes me that these questions are very consistent from year to year. After hearing many of the same questions about wine over and over again from attendees, I began to form a distinct way of teaching the class that is both entertaining and informative. Everything I speak about in the basics class is to succinctly answer common questions that seem to create a hurdle between wine consumer and opening a bottle of wine. Of course, to be honest, I'm also a total ham in front of a crowd, and I love the thrill and challenge of introducing the difficult subject of wine to people who are curious about it!

The book is made up of a series of quotes, observations, and anecdotes that together create a series of vignettes that make up a story, almost a drama of my world in wine. I'm not sure how many times I've gotten the question, "How long should I age a wine?" But I've gotten this next question and similar ones, almost as many times. "Do American wines have more sulfites than European wines?" When I get these types of questions, I don't just answer them. I try to give the wine consumer a different perspective—how will the answer to a question improve your life? OK, a glass of wine can't solve all the world's ills, but certainly a better-informed wine consumer will feel more confident and may even make wine a part of his or her daily meals.

Let the story begin, and beware—I really do drink on the job!

Charlie "I Drink on the Job" Adler

INTRODUCTION—I Drink On the Job

At a French Embassy wine tasting I was holding:

French Security: Monsieur, a woman is stuck inside zee bathroom stall.

Charlie: "Well, then let her out!"

French Security: "Unfortunately, it is in the men's room."

Charlie: "Uhh, OK, break down the door."

French Security: "We are not sure, but a man may be in the stall with her."

Charlie: "Ohhh."

Woman at a cocktail party at the New Zealand Embassy in Washington, DC, 1999:

Woman: "So what do you do for a living?"

Charlie: "I'm a full-time wine professional. I run TasteDC."

Woman: "That's very unusual in this town...what is your favorite wine?"

Charlie: "Well, of course, I like the crisp Sauvignon Blancs they make in New Zealand. They're really excellent with the oysters we're being served. But I like a wide range of wines, from French Burgundy, their wonderful Pinot Noirs, to a really good, robust red Zinfandel. Right now, I'm really getting into California Cabernets, but my tastes change all the time!"

Woman smiles nervously, and changes the subject.

Scene 1: Setting the Stage

Charlie Adler, TasteDC's president and the speaker for *Wine Basics 101*, appears at a downtown hotel about one hour before the class is to begin. He walks around the room making mental checks to see if everything is in place: Looking at each round table—four wine glasses per person to the right—check; one water glass filled with ice water—check; a spit bucket on the table for waste wine—check; sufficient cheese and crackers at the center of the table—check; one flute per person for the aperitif—check; enough tables and chairs to accommodate everyone—check. Once the volunteers arrive to assist in pouring the wines, taking coats, and assisting Charlie in the event (they get to participate and drink as well!), Charlie turns his focus to the event and his notes.

Charlie ponders several questions: How did the last class, go? What engaged the audience the most? Was it stories and anecdotes, or was it just hard facts about wine? Did he make any mistakes or snafus? Did he say something the audience either didn't get or found offensive or difficult to understand? What will the class be like? Will it be mostly twenty-somethings, or will there be an age mix? What can he do to make this the best class ever? What can he give attendees that will be memorable for a lifetime or at least help them feel more confident about their wine decisions? Where is his glass. He needs a drink!

He walks up to the bottles of white wine chilling and the reds standing up on the table in the order they will be poured, and he begins to open them, some with screw tops, others needing a corkscrew. He pours a few drops of each wine in his glass, swirls and sniffs to see if the wines are fine or if they have gone bad. Each wine has the different characteristics and aromas that he expects and that bring up past memories, normally of food and wine pairings, or trips he made in wine country. He writes down two or three notes per wine on his tasting sheet.

Charlie greets all the volunteers, his regular faithful ones, with a personal greeting and asks about what they've been up to; new volunteers are greeted as a group. Normally, he engages the volunteers in a conversation about their wine backgrounds and reminds them that they will, in fact, get to participate and taste all the wines, seated with everyone else. He demonstrates for new volunteers how to quickly pour about one and a half ounces of wine into each glass without spilling, and each volunteer gets a practice glass. Once volunteers are given their duties to either greet or seat people or to pour wine, he makes sure that every seat has a tasting sheet with the list of nine wines on it. He goes back to his notes and his speech, reminding himself that there's a lot to cover in only a bit over two hours.

As the time gets nearer to the start of the event, usually a few minutes after 7:00 p.m., Charlie closes his eyes and imagines the event, the people, the wine, and the audience vibe. He tries to make a mental picture of a room of people in harmony, relating to his experiences, listening to his explanations, laughing at his antics, and possibly discovering something real and new. He wants everyone to walk out a better wine consumer and with better knowledge and confidence. A small percentage of them, maybe 10 to 15 percent of the people, will come back to TasteDC events and become "regulars."

Good evening, everyone. Welcome to TasteDC's *Wine Basics 101* Class. My name is Charlie Adler, I'm the president of TasteDC, and my motto is <long pause> I drink on the job!

For the last twelve years, I've been creating and organizing wine events at TasteDC: from the very popular *Wine Basics 101* class to functions at embassies and many varied food events, as well, such as cooking classes. It's a unique job. I'm sort of living the 'dream,' but not all is fun and games at work. There are many pitfalls I have to deal with, from difficult embassy officials to the reality of economics and competition. Yes, TasteDC is my full-time job. I scrape out a living trying to entertain and educate people with the wonders of wine and food, but things are changing all the time. I never know what to expect.

One observation that I can't get past is that anyone can learn about wine. There is no special characteristic or knowledge base a person needs to understand this seemingly complex beverage. All anyone needs is a willingness to learn and keep an open mind. I want to motivate you to start drinking wine, not just once a month or once a week, but I mean every day, or as often as you deem possible. I want to make choosing wine in a restaurant a cinch, because tasting and understanding nuances in wine won't be a problem, and naming the five red wine grapes of Bordeaux will be second nature. Just like the sixteen thousand attendees at the popular *Wine Basics 101* class, you will start drinking wine with intelligence and confidence, even before you finish the book. So, let's get started with the basics, with a little about the number one wine class in Washington, DC, twelve years in a row and a bit about me...oh, and you should definitely pour yourself a glass of wine, right about...now!

How many people here have never been to a wine class before? (About half the hands of the audience go up.) Well congratulations, you've finally made the move to learn about wine. Learning about wine is a journey that will continue for the rest of your life.

I find stories engage people more than lectures, so that's how I teach *Wine Basics 101*, the core class at TasteDC. Every time I teach this class, I add new material and see how the audience reacts. Sometimes, I try new tactics, like the time I asked 150 attendees at the class to draw their favorite foods with a pen on paper, or other times when I talked about various scenes from the movie *Sideways*. I admit I use many different methods with one goal in mind—to engage the audience, so that they will open up to new experiences. To me, teaching *Wine Basics 101* isn't just teaching a wine class. It goes much deeper into the person's psyche. I want the attendees to *experience* wine—completely!

Two Guys on a Wine Country Road Trip Made a Big Difference

In *Wine Basics 101*, attendance has gone up and down over the years, but the biggest effect on sales was the movie *Sideways*.

After the movie first played in 2004, average attendance went from around seventy people to well over a hundred, sometimes one hundred fifty-plus people attended a class, and this event was held every other month. The movie really struck a chord with the twenty-something crowd, and wine became very hip. Since that time, sales have leveled off, closer to fifty people per class, but the interest in wine both in DC and the United States. has noticeably increased since I started in 1997. Wine, as part of the American lifestyle, is here to stay. I'll drink to that!

Who Are These People?

Probably my biggest challenge in an introductory wine class is to approach a widely diverse audience. Washington, DC, has a large African-American population, but otherwise, it is very transient, with people coming from all over America and all over the world; DC is a true melting pot. Speaking to such a varied group of people poses a big challenge, so I'm forced to speak in broad generalizations or, as I like to say, "big brush strokes," that usually work most of the time. For example, I talk about the French people and their interest in food, wine, and culture, or I talk subtle wine distinctions. If you really think about it, an "American" isn't one type of person or nationality; we are defined by our diversity. What we all have in common is our culture, which is pretty much the interests we share in movies, TV, restaurants, and other public venues. The difference between, say, a Texan and a person from Minnesota is vast, but most likely both of them have been to the same movies and eaten at some of the same chain restaurants like Ruby Tuesdays. They may have gone to similar colleges or been in the U.S. military. There is such a thing as an American "persona" and, frankly, it's very different than a French persona.

Before We Taste, a Little Background on Charlie Adler

Setting: on a private jet tour of food and wine destinations throughout Europe. Charlie is relaxing on the back of a plane at about 9:00 a.m. thinking about the four-course lunch ahead, wine tasting, and then the six-course dinner in Burgundy, France.

English Flight Attendant (walks by Charlie and notices that his two mini-Champagne flutes are out of Champagne): "Charlie, care for any more Champagne?"

Charlie: (thinks for a moment, then replies): "Absolutely!"

I've had some pretty awesome experiences in my twelve years of being a wine professional. Probably the high point was when I was hired by a private luxury jet tour company in 2001 to fly around Europe on a first-class private jet, sleep at three- and four-star hotels, eat four- to eight-course meals for lunch and dinner (with wine of course!), and enjoy being treated like royalty—things are not all bad at TasteDC! Obviously, this is the exception and not the rule to life as a wine professional. Mostly, I organize wine courses and cooking classes and arrange with hotels and restaurants to hold them a few times a week in the DC area. Personally, I come from a pretty average background, from a small town in Pennsylvania. Nothing about my early life really suggests that I would do anything more than take over the family real estate business.

A lot of people who get started in the wine business have a wine "epiphany," and the story usually goes that they were sitting in a fancy restaurant or travelling to some foreign country when they caught the wine bug. My epiphany actually started when I was thirteen years old and my dad let me choose the wine and open it for all future family dinners. I finally had my first serious adult responsibility—I had become a man!

Hometown Boy

I was brought up in Harrisburg, Pennsylvania, a small town, which is actually the capital as well. The first thing most people say when you mention Harrisburg is, "Yes, I've driven through it," but unfortunately, very few people actually stop there. It's simply on the way to so many other places. The best part of living in Harrisburg was that it was close to other cities: two hours from Philadelphia and Washington, DC, about four hours from New York City. I really enjoyed growing up in a small town—the familiarity with so many people, the relaxed, slower-paced lifestyle, and frankly the ability to create a lot of trouble and get away with it!

One thing that always stands out for me is that my parents were both interested in all things culinary, and we often ate out at fine dining restaurants. I don't want to mislead you; my mother was a pretty awful cook (As the joke goes: "What does a Jewish woman make for dinner? Reservations!"), and what we mostly ate during the week was grilled steak with lemon pepper and butter or chicken broiled with, you guessed it, lemon pepper and butter. Almost every vegetable I ever ate came out of a can (I still love Le Sueur Early Peas!) or was cooked to death, except for the infamous iceberg lettuce, the only kind of lettuce ever offered—I grew up in the days before romaine and mache lettuce had caught on. The best experiences I had with food growing up were at local restaurants like Lombardos, which served rack of lamb, sole meuniere, and other classic American-Italian dishes like veal parmigiana, and of course, spaghetti and meatballs, which came with every dish. We had a well-represented Greek community in the area, and most restaurants were Greek owned, so early on I enjoyed gyros, moussaka, spanakopita, and toropitas (spinach and cheese pies in phyllo). Chinese was the downtown Canton Inn with egg rolls, wonton soup, BBQ spare ribs, and shrimp, chicken, or beef chow mein, until the spicy Szechuan restaurant opened up in the early '70s. Let's just say, I couldn't wait to go out to a restaurant to eat!

My father taught me two rules when he handed the corkscrew over to me: "White with fish and red with meat," and "Always sniff the cork when it is offered to you." I now know both these rules were wrong.

Pennsylvania is a liquor-control state. This means that all wine, beer, and spirits are completely controlled by a state bureaucracy; even the liquor stores are owned and run by the state. With a few exceptions for beer sales, the only way to purchase alcoholic beverages was to run to the local liquor store and hope they had something on the shelf that was of decent quality, which you could actually swallow without choking. In the 1970s, this meant that my father mostly brought to the dinner table Mateus, Blue Nun, Yago Sangria, Great Western Sparkling "Champagne," and the occasional French Pouilly Fuissé. Risking purchasing one of the cheap imported wines often meant that the red wines were so bitter and tannic that we couldn't even drink them at a meal. They ended up down the drain.

Charlie is nineteen years old with an eighteen-year-old date back in the early '80s at a fine dining restaurant just outside Harrisburg, Pennsylvania. The drinking age back then was eighteen. The wine list is handed to Charlie, who chooses a white wine, which he's never heard of, which is presented by the sommelier at the table. Charlie tastes, approves, and it's poured for both his date and him.

Eighteen-year-old date: "I don't like this wine. It's sour."

Charlie: "It seems OK. Do you want something else?

Eighteen-year-old date: "Yes, Riunite. Do they have Riunite?"

Charlie: "Probably. It's pretty much available everywhere."

Charlie calls over the sommelier: "We'd like to send this wine back. My date would prefer the Riunite."

Sommelier takes the wine and returns with Riunite, shows the label to Charlie, pours a little for a taste, Charlie approves, and the sommelier pours wine in both glasses.

I think everyone has an embarrassing wine story, something they either feel uncomfortable talking about or even a bit ashamed of. This seems to be pretty normal for most folks. I've put my foot in my mouth and seen and heard other people do the same thing many times. Sometimes, trying to be just too proper or correct actually intensifies a mistake and makes everyone uncomfortable and uneasy. The most difficult time for anyone to deal with a wine decision is usually ordering out at a fine-dining restaurant, particularly when there is a sommelier with one of those shiny medallions around her neck—the ultimate intimidation, which gets twice as bad when the wine list is put on the table; the list often weighs almost ten pounds! It contains hundreds of wines in various categories that you've most likely never heard of, and some often cost hundreds of dollars or more. What about the vintage? The same wine might come in 1998, 2000, 2001, 2004, and there are different prices for each, what to do? And what about pairing the wine with the food? What if everyone is eating a totally different dish, how do you choose one wine?

At TasteDC, I do as many events with food as I do with wine. Wine is meant to be served with food—period. In European countries, wine is often just sitting on the table either at home or in a restaurant. Wine is also relatively inexpensive, particularly in France, Spain, and Italy; I mean a Coca-Cola often costs more!

When I was growing up in Harrisburg, the only people who regularly drank wine for dinner were either foreigners or considered very eccentric. Back then, most people ordered cocktails in a restaurant. Wine was still pretty exotic and, often, the quality was poor, or it was dearly expensive. My parents came from the Depression generation, and their peers generally pooh-poohed anyone who had airs or who tried to act sophisticated. Even food wasn't meant to be fussed about too much. Meat was in the middle of the plate and some overcooked veggies were placed on the side of the plate, with maybe a cold iceberg salad. This was standard. Sunday was a treat. We ate Chinese! Drinking wine was about being "fancy"—it was for going out to eat or for a special occasion. Pairing wine with food was unheard of; the choices were so limited at the local liquor store and even at restaurants that you simply drank the best wine you could afford with any food.

Brie and Chardonnay

My first experiences with the social aspect of wine were at family and small gatherings with my parents and their friends in the '70s. This was the era of so-called "gourmet" products like Camembert cheese, fancy mustards (you may remember the infamous Grey Poupon commercial), and anything French. Whether it was influenced by Julia Child or not is difficult to say, but everything French became the rage! More fancy French restaurants opened up in town, and heavy cream sauces began to appear. Whether the food was authentic or not made no difference; status for the upper-middle-class families was gained by entertaining with French food and wine. This was the era of Brie and Chardonnay—there seemed to be an unending number of small gatherings where cold oaky Chardonnay was served with the infamous round of brie. Some served the cheese firm, others runny, but the wine was always served refrigerator chilled. What I remember most about the wine was that it was rich, buttery, and oaky. My impression was that all things "French" meant heavy, creamy foods and weighty wines.

Nawlins Foodie

My interest in wine continued in college when I attended Tulane University, both undergraduate school from 1980 to 1984, with a philosophy/history double major, and graduate school, in the business program from 1984 to 1986. New Orleans was eye-opening for me because the spices and style of cooking completely elevated my taste buds and intense interest in food and wine. I can still remember attending a wine tasting in graduate school and how little everyone knew about wine. The person explaining the wine came from a wealthy family, and the assumption was that he knew about wine because of his background. All of the MBA candidates wanted an edge at their job interviews, so most of us thought that knowing about wine might help us if we were invited to a corporate meal as part of the interviewing process. Back then, the business philosophy was that a good candidate should order a steak and bourbon to show he or she was decisive and a strong candidate!

The New Orleans food scene was always unique, with Creole and Cajun cuisine, but I also noticed an interest in consuming wine with meals. New Orleanians didn't make a big fuss about drinking with a meal—beer, wine, or even a cocktail was fine—people just enjoyed their drink! I began to experiment tasting different wines, going to wine tastings and purchasing French Burgundies from a local store. I had no formal education. I just began to taste and experiment: one night a French red with Chinese food, another night a Chardonnay with gumbo. It was all new and exciting to me.

Much of the food in New Orleans has flavor and sauce. For example, when you order a sandwich (pronounced "samwich") you are asked if you want it "dressed," which means with lettuce, onion, and tomato, but sometimes mustard and mayo too. Even a barbecued pork sandwich would often have mayonnaise added to it, another dimension of fat and flavor! The one thing about New Orleans food is that it is never dry, like the food I grew up on, and never bland. There is always spice, sometimes hot, but sometimes just flavorful. Whether you order a po'boy sandwich dressed, or go to Commander's Palace and have a fancy French meal, the food in New Orleans is explosively tasteful, with garlic, green peppers, onions, and spices—flavors I had never truly experienced at home in Harrisburg. Garlic was all but forbidden from Mama Adler's kitchen, and onions were rarely used; spices dried up in the cupboard over the stove after ten years of non-use.

Get Real...Estate

I moved to Washington, DC, in 1987, pretty fresh out of Tulane as a gung ho commercial real estate agent, ready to lease office buildings, warehouses, or anything that came my way. I spent the next ten years in and out of firms, always wondering why I never seemed to do as well as I should. Something seemed to be missing in my life, and that was a passion for my work. My father and two generations before him had been successful at real estate in Harrisburg, so I just assumed that I would make it big in DC. After ten years of struggling just to make a living, I had come to a conclusion about myself—money simply wasn't that important to me. I never felt comfortable going after a buck. I needed to have the whole story behind the deal. I couldn't just lease a space to a restaurant. I wanted to know how they ran their business, what their menu would look like, how they approached food costs, and all the details of running a business.

I wanted to own my own business, but selling widgets or running a business wasn't enough. I wanted something that was just plain more intellectually involving—oh, and lots of fun!

Party Guy

I organized singles parties in DC in the early '90s starting with backyard barbecues, with kegs of beer at my group house on Dent Place, NW, soon followed by Sunday evening parties at various clubs. I would get one hundred to three hundred people and usually charged $10 to attend, so they were more about having fun than a commercial success. In 1997, I threw a free party at my Georgetown house and invited everyone to a wine tasting; bring your own wine was requested, but no other information was mentioned. About sixty people came with bottles of wine, and we opened and poured them. Even though there was a wine speaker, by the time she got up on the chair to talk about the wine, the affair was so social and raucous that nobody could hear a word she said. Everyone was simply talking, drinking, and mingling!

The party was so popular that many attendees told me I should make a living organizing wine events. This concept was pretty new at the time, but there were a few other groups in the area that were organizing wine events, so I began to do a little research. After attending about ten wine-related events, from introduction to wine tasting to wine dinners (and also a vodka tasting at the Russian Embassy, where I had a few too many shots and was asked to vacate!), I figured I could make a go of it. All I needed to do was convince some of my friends and fellow partygoers to attend. I threw my first wine tasting at a restaurant on M Street, NW, just outside of Georgetown in DC and had nearly a hundred attendees and, thus, TasteDC was born.

Beginning of Taste

If this is your first event with TasteDC, let me mention that we are more than just about wine. Food is really an important component of what I do, from cooking classes, how to make pizza, to introducing people to matching food and wine. Let's not exclude beer and spirits. I organize the DC Rum Festival, Whisky Festival, and we do Sake too. TasteDC is here to help you with your eat and drink.

I've organized nearly a thousand events in the twelve years of TasteDC's existence from wine classes to big Embassy shindigs. DC is a unique city in that we have almost every country's embassy in or around our city. I've organized many wine tastings at the French Embassy as well as the German, Spanish, Croatian, Argentinean, Bolivian, Bulgarian, Australian, Hungarian, and South African embassies. I've also held cultural events at the Lithuanian, Polish, Ukrainian, Uzbeki, and Czech Republic embassies, as well as been associated with events at both the Italian and Russian embassies. The most dramatic occurrence (other than the woman stuck in the French Embassy men's room mentioned at the beginning of the book) was my plan to hold a cultural event of Cuban food, mojitos, and cigars at the Cuban Interest Section (Cuba does not have an embassy, but the Swiss Embassy represents them in the United States) on Sixteenth Street. This was right around the time of the first Baltimore Orioles game with the Cubans in 2000, and I received a huge negative response from the Cuban-American interests in the United States, including a scary letter from the U.S. State Department essentially telling me I could be arrested, and one e-mail death threat from a Miami protester. We cancelled the event, but as they say, all publicity is good publicity; I'm still in business today!

Embassy Events

Washington, DC, is a unique city in that almost every country's embassy is here, and many of them hold events for the public where wine is often served.

I'm not sure how many times I've been to the French Embassy for a wine tasting, but probably more than all the other embassies combined. The French actually have a separate organization just to manage events at the La Maison Francaise, and it's an attractive white marble '70s style space with high ceilings and lots of natural sunlight. Through TasteDC, I've organized and been involved with many events there including the Mushroom and Wine Festival, Tour du Fromage, Seven-Course Gala Dinner in Honor of The Third Millennium, Bastille Day Celebration (where I introduced Warren Brown of Cake Love and the show *Sugar Rush* on Food Network to Duff Goldman, who later had his own show on Food Network, *Ace of Cakes*), Le Beaujolais Nouveau, and countless other gatherings, including one of the largest events I have ever organized when over eight hundred people attended the Champagne Festival.

Although the French themselves hold many wine tastings and food events at their own embassy, I brought a new American perspective to embassy wine tastings, and many organizations throughout the United States have imitated TasteDC's events over the last decade. In a very small way, TasteDC pioneered the balanced food and wine event where cuisine is equally as important as is the wine. Wine and food events are evolving with the American consumer, and as cooking schools pop up all over the United States and interest grows in better eating and wine, TasteDC will continue to innovate. If America can make wine as good as any in the world, I believe we can make cheeses, chocolate, charcuterie, and any other artisanal product just as well as any other country. Rather than just copy the European model, we innovate by finding what makes our background, geography, and perspective unique, and in the process, possibly reinvent new tastes.

Thank You, Food Network!

One of the biggest changes in attendees at *Wine Basics 101* the last few years has been the interest in more than just wine, but food as well. It seems celebrity chefs have gained everyone's attention, and the quality of restaurants has really increased significantly here in DC in the last few years. Food and wine were meant for each other.

Food Network has changed the way I do business at TasteDC, and I've added more specialty cooking classes and events around food than ever before. As I like to say, "Food is more important than wine." You *have to* eat; drinking wine is simply an added pleasure, but an important one. The connection between producing great quality artisanal foods, such as cheese and charcuterie, is very similar to the production of great craft beers and small producer wines—the hands-on character of production not only affects the quality but often the taste, as well. I won't say that a smaller producer's product is necessarily "better" than a large, industrially manufactured wine or food, but by supporting small artisans, you are making a statement that you care about supporting innovation in taste and flavors. Even something as small as the quality of milk can affect the final cheese, just as in wine, the location and the way the grapes are grown and harvested and eventually vinified can affect the final outcome.

DC Foodie

My current main focus of events at TasteDC is wine classes, small group tours of local producers, and learning how to make their artisan products. I have a relationship with various local beef purveyors and chocolate, cheese, pizza, and other small manufacturers of specialty gourmet products. I'm a big *locavore* so I try to support as many local producers of quality products as I can, and there is no event too strange—just recently, we took a group to a chorizo making 101 class in Fairfax County, Virginia, where we learned how chorizo was made, the different varieties, and how to cook with chorizo. Wine and beer were also served. I mean most of my classes include some kind of unique pairings. The future of TasteDC is to discover and promote new food and beverage artisans in the Washington, DC, area. I really want to put the "taste" in DC!

What makes a good or great wine? I'm not really sure, but I like to look at the question a bit differently. If you had one day to live, what would you choose as your last meal? Mine would be a grilled cheeseburger with crispy French fries, and yes, ketchup too!

Show me a wine rule, and I'll show you a way to break it and get more pleasure out of wine.

Charlie Adlerisms

I like to take a standard fact or truism in wine and create a new way of looking at it. I could simply say that a particular wine tastes *oaky* or *tannic*, but I'd rather mention some other significant factor that relates to this experience. Maybe I'll mention that the wine has a chocolaty note or that oak reminds me of barbeque because of the smoke. I also don't mind a little controversy; in fact, I think the wine world needs to be shaken up a bit. I'm mostly influenced by the iconoclasts in the wine world like Randall Graham of Bonny Doon Winery and Alice Feiring, who tend to go against the popular corporate "do as everyone else does, and you'll do fine," and make people wake up and question wine. When I'm teaching wine and cooking classes, I always enjoy posing questions and thoughts to the attendees that make them question what it is that makes a wine good, what makes the ingredients of a dish work, or why it is that Americans seem to have a hard time understanding taste.

Many of my quotes in this book and in real life come from my deep-seated need to get people to understand—I don't want to just teach, I want to change people's lives by giving them a new direction or a new way of looking at the world of food and wine. I question every fact I've been taught about wine and all hearsay, because often it's just plain wrong. For the longest time, wine industry types and educators talked about how you could taste the soil in a glass of wine, even though this was pure conjecture and mostly nonsense. I love to introduce this idea to the wine class and then pose the dilemma—what if you can't taste the soil? Does this make a difference? I don't want a group of people writing down and memorizing every word of alleged wisdom I pose to them. I really just want people to enjoy a nice bottle of wine, hopefully with a meal. As I told my Tulane alumni group a few years back, "Go figure that a guy who spent six years in New Orleans perfecting his ability to drink and party ended up in the wine business!"

Exercise 1: Think about your first pleasant experience with wine—this should preferably be a memory from when you were younger. Close your eyes and take a few minutes to imagine the people around you at the time, the wine itself, its container, and any sounds, sights, or smells you associate with the mental picture. Try to picture what type of event was occurring: a celebration, a special occasion, or any other details about the moment. Did you taste the wine or did you simply watch others enjoy it? Think about how you felt in general and your first associations with the experience. Try to make it vivid in your mind by accentuating the images, sounds, and smells. This is your "Original Wine Experience."

---

1 WINE BASICS 101—Wine with Class

At Embassy of Argentina 2009

Woman (walks up to table where there are eight different Argentine wines for pouring): "Which is your best wine?"

Charlie: "If you had eight children, would you choose a favorite?"

It's About You

Two things determine the American wine drinker: high income and advanced education. Congratulations—pat yourself on the back for being a part of this adventure!

A feel-good statement is frankly my way of getting the audience on my side. I know the reality is that wine makes Americans very uncomfortable. It's sort of the adult thing you do when you reach a certain success level early in your career, but it's often a chore. After hearing so many of the same questions about wine over and over again at the introductory class for the last twelve years, I know that Americans want to know about wine.

You want to understand why it tastes a certain way. Can you figure out all of its nuances? What is the best wine? How much should you spend? Do the legs of wine mean anything? The conclusion—Americans simply aren't very comfortable with the "concept" of wine, but they drink it heartily nonetheless.

Americans are very confused by wine. It's the only hobby where people think they're supposed to know everything about it *before* they start.

What is it about wine that is so confusing? A farmer grows grapes, presses the juice, ferments it, maybe puts it in barrel for a while, and then bottles it, and it somehow gets to the store or restaurant. All you have to do as a consumer is choose the right bottle for the occasion, pay the man, and enjoy or leave with a tasty bottle of wine. Shouldn't be hard, no?

"How many people in here drink more than once a month (most hands get raised), once a week (about half the room has hands up), two or three times a week (about 20 percent of the people have their hands up), every day (a small percentage have their hands up), every meal (all hands go down, mine goes up)?"

I have a goal in mind at TasteDC and that's to get people to drink more often and feel better about their wine-purchasing decisions. You don't need to know a lot about wine to start drinking it. A few handy rules and a basic understanding of how it's made and where it fits in with food go a long way. This brings me directly to the central challenge of this book and why I think this is not just another wine book.

Central Premise

Americans believe that there is a right and wrong wine choice and they don't want to make a mistake. This is why Americans put too much emphasis on wine experts, expensive wine accessories, and wine education. The solution is much simpler: wine comes from European culture and, over there, it is simply part of the meal. Wine is meant to be consumed with food!

This is really a two-part dilemma: 1) Americans are very confused by wine, and 2) wine has been a part of European culture for centuries and is simply part of the meal. I'll reiterate these points throughout this book, just as I do in the wine class. The question is, why are Americans so confused? What is it about identifying, purchasing, and consuming wine that is so complicated? Why do I constantly get the question, "What is your favorite wine?" but no one ever seems to listen to the answer I give. It's almost as if Americans are so stressed out about the prospect of dealing with wine that they'd rather simply put it on someone else's shoulders, and then they can simply say someone told them so!

There is no best wine or wine that fits every occasion or application. Frankly, most Americans in blind tastings choose cheaper wines over more expensive ones! (Goldstein, Robin. *The Wine Trial.* Austin: Fearless Critic Media, 2008.)

So what do people do when a subject confuses them and they want to know more? They generally rely on an expert's advice, or maybe a book or other quality resource, and maybe they begin to study the subject. On the face of it, this seems very reasonable, but ironically, this is not what most people end up doing! Most people seem to pick up information from a friend, who knew someone, who said...well, there are plenty of indirect sources for information, right? In all actuality, even experts give bad advice—too much bad advice because they often don't know the answer to wine questions either or they have outdated information.

So learning about wine is very frustrating, with bad information from many different sources—so whom do you trust? Of course you can find a wine critic like Robert Parker or critics from *Wine Spectator* and simply follow their recommendations. They have a high trust factor and are very knowledgeable, so they're reliable. Still, the problem remains. At what point do you trust your own opinion? Most people will watch a movie even if some wine critics pan the movie—this is because Americans know movies. You watch them all the time. They are part of American culture. Some people like drama, some like action flicks, some like "chick flicks," but both the producers of the movies and you, the consumers, have a good idea what to expect. With wine, it's a black hole for many, simply a product where the language of producer, wholesaler, representative, and retailer doesn't translate very well to your lifestyle. You like a sweet or oaky wine—sure, there are plenty of them, but there's so much more added complexity to the equation: do you want a domestic or foreign wine, do you know what year (vintage) is best, have you thought about your food choices, do you want an organic wine, what about sparkling, what about your guests, will they like it? And I almost forgot, the question blurts out unexpectedly: "What makes a good wine?"

Wine Rules

There is only one rule in wine: if you like it, it's good! No matter what I tell you about it or who tries to convince you otherwise, ultimately, your sense of taste will determine if the wine is a keeper or a loser.

So the problem is solved. You can stop reading the book and go on your happy way choosing delicious wines for your home, business meals, and entertainment, and you will be able to hold your head high, no more embarrassing mistaken wine judgments! Well, maybe not so easy. I mean most wine stores carry five hundred plus different selections of wine, and there are literally tens of thousands of wines produced every year. Most people take the easy route—they simply choose a wine based on a price they want to pay, say less than $15, and then they find a label that attracts them in some way. Maybe it's a pretty picture of a bicycle or a very distinguished fancy label. You can read the shelf-talker, which tells you normally the wine critic's score and a few points about the wine, and maybe it even mentions the food pairing "goes delicious with cheese, fish, and chili."

European Culture

American culture and European culture are very different pertaining to both food and wine. In Europe, especially in countries like France, Spain, and Italy, wine is simply a part of the meal; the bottle of wine is on the table. All income levels and groups enjoy wine, from truck drivers to the wealthy; it simply is a part of most meals.

So Americans want to enjoy wine and understand everything about it, but they want to be sure they're making the right choice. Over in Europe, most people are brought up with it from a very young age, and it doesn't even represent a luxury product; it's just something around the table primarily for lunch and dinner, and even children are sometimes offered a diluted glass (normally mixed with water) as part of their meal. It makes a lot of sense—in France, wine making is a significant generator of jobs in their economy, and it is a part of their customs and way of life. In America, wine is more so of a luxury product, for a few reasons. The largest segment of growth in the wine business here is wine that costs $10 or more a bottle. The average bottle of wine purchased in a DC restaurant is going to set you back more like $40—before tax and tip, so this is a significant cost. As I said before, congratulations, if you're a wine drinker in the United States and you're reading this book. Most likely you have a nice, high household income!

My premise for the book and the *Wine Basics 101* class is that wine in America is considered a cultural activity, often similar to attending an opera, ballet, or symphony. These are activities that many Europeans again were brought up with and don't consider to be always a prestigious affair, but in America, these are the activities of the elite and those who want to be part of their lifestyle. Don't get me wrong—many men have been pulled by the collar to unwillingly attend a $200/person opera at the Kennedy Center, but I think it's pretty clear that only white-collar, high-income profiles normally attend these events. The good news: more Americans are catching the wine bug, and the demographics are broadening for wine consumption. I doubt we will see many truck drivers and blue-collar types pick up the habit in this country, but it really is a shame, because wine from the European view just makes a meal so much more interesting and delicious, and it beats simply opening a cold one!

Wine = Booze

America's love/hate relationship with alcoholic beverages of all kinds probably stems from the outdated thinking that alcohol is alcohol, no matter what form it comes in. When I went out to dinner as a kid, I still remember many adults that had a few too many gin and tonics or whiskies before, during, and after meals, and how my parents looked down on those over-imbibers. Wine was a sign of sophistication in my youth, not something you overdrank, unless it was Thunderbird or wine coolers.

The way most people purchase wines in a store or supermarket is they think about what price they want to spend, and then they look for a label they like.

Because of all the confusion and mystery about wine, most people don't have a strong criterion for choosing a wine. As people often tell me, they just walk in the store, think of a price they want to pay, and choose a label or wine region that seems to look nice. Some wine purchasers also use reviews from magazines and wine articles, but the problem often is that stores don't always have these wines in stock. The wine industry has known for years how perplexed Americans can be with the vino purchase, and many companies have given what you love: labels that are colorful and humorous at a price point around $10/bottle, where you don't have to think much—the infamous "cute purchase." Nothing is wrong with purchasing wine like this, but for a regular wine drinker, which I hope you become after reading this book, you need a bit more information. The question is what information is important and what tidbits of data are simply not worth your time.

Wine Discomfort

Most people who first get started out in wine look for guidance from a wine professional or a publication. This way, no one can question their judgment; they can always say, "Well, this is what (name a wine professional) said.

Because of Americans' discomfort with choosing a wine, many prefer to use a review they've read in either a lifestyle publication, on the Internet, or in wine articles. It's easier to let someone else make a decision for you; that way you can put a bottle in your supermarket cart and be on your merry way. This almost makes purchasing wine stress free, but you still have to be able to swallow it and enjoy it. What happens if you simply don't enjoy the wine, even though the wine critic told you it was good?

Americans are very comfortable shopping for various products. Take shoes for example: ask any woman if she knows how to shop for shoes and what her criterion is, and she just knows. When two women get together, they seem to understand shoes, what clothes they match with, what's in style, who was wearing them, etc. Purchasing wine is a totally different story.

This always gets curious looks and laughs from the audience, but it rings so true. Shopping is an experience that many people find entertaining, maybe even exhilarating, but only so for products that we understand. Americans price-comparison shop, search for fashionable or attractive items, or simply shop for staples. It's only when people decide to shop outside their comfort zone that the experience becomes totally different. Shopping for wine seems to increase people's stress level, because it is important to the consumer on so many levels—purchasing wine confers on the shopper a certain expertise and, with that, comes status. If you know something about wine, it suggests that you may have traveled to foreign countries and enjoyed wine, you have visited wineries, or possibly that you often eat at fine dining establishments. There's nothing wrong with status seeking, which is why wine has grown so popular in the United States; the early adopters have given way to the wine newbie masses, but choosing the wine still seems problematic. Why can't Americans figure out what's in the bottle by simply tasting it?

Americans don't seem to trust their sense of taste with wine. If you like steak, then you don't need anyone to tell you if it's good or not; you've enjoyed steak since you were young and you know what you like—medium or medium-rare, one-inch thick, two-inch, rib eye, filet or strip—even if someone else disagrees. We have no experience with wine as a culture, so we seek peer approval.

Accessorize

This leads me into the accessory debate—what do you need to purchase before you can enjoy wine? Lots of glassware, say that fancy stemware you see in all the wine magazines touting the benefits of "superior aeration" and "accentuate the nuances," or just a simple red or white wine glass, maybe a flute for sparkling wine? Should you purchase that $49.99 rabbit "ears" corkscrew contraption or simply buy a classic "waiter's friend" for around $6.99? How about a wine thermometer, wine stopper(s), champagne cork remover, decanter, aeration device, or some other contraption that will add to your bill even before you open the bottle? What do you need, what is necessary, and what is simply a waste of money? And do you need the best?

Back to Taste...

How can you develop an appreciation for food or wine? What is it about a dish, say a nicely grilled piece of salmon with a nice sauce on top, which you either like or don't like? Does the type of salmon matter? How about the waters it was fished from? Does that add flavor, or is farm-raised actually your preference? Do you like butter in your sauce, or do you prefer cream? Maybe you think olive oil with a touch of herbs and garlic is better. What about "blackened," how is that for you? What does a salmon taste like? Is it rich or oily or fishy, and what do you mean by "fishy"? Do you mean aromas of the shore or that it smells spoiled?

My goal at TasteDC is to get people to trust their taste, but this is a complicated matter, especially with people who are just learning. The good news is that Americans learn very quickly, and this has become obvious in just the last five years after *Sideways*, where some of the questions at my events are so good, that neither the presenter nor I always know the answers. Americans are picking up the wine bug, so let's get you started in the right direction; it's time to taste!

Just Say It!

Americans like wines they can pronounce:
"shar-duh-NAY," "mair-LOE." These are easy...
"Guh-VERTS-tra-MEE-ner" will never happen!

If a wine is easy to pronounce, you will most likely remember it and, thus, you will more likely be willing to buy it in the future. Ironically, European wines often have difficult names to pronounce and often the grape (varietal) is not put on the label, thus creating one more headache in the purchasing decision. Many Americans often assume (and this tends to be an older demographic, so things are changing rapidly) that only French or Italian wines are any good, so they want to learn as much as possible about these wines. Even the French are now starting to change their labels for the American market.

Rely on Critics

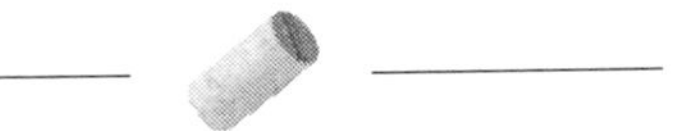

If a movie critic reviewed a movie and said it was not good, would this stop you from seeing the movie? Probably not—it would be a factor, but you would probably ask your friends or other people who had seen it. Most Americans know something about movies. Wine is a whole different story.

Many Americans rely on wine critics to help them choose a wine—it's probably the number one most important marketing element for a wine and, ultimately, for the retail store. If you aren't sure what wine to choose, you can pick up many publications such as the *Wine Advocate* or the *Wine Spectator* and you can get your favorite wine critic to choose a wine for you. Wine critics are much more influential than probably any other critic that Americans follow, for one reason: Americans don't know much about wine. It's so much easier to simply choose wines that have a ninety-point or higher score from your favorite critic than it is to actually learn and choose wine for yourself. Although this is a simple, effective method, it doesn't satisfy my criterion for a good wine choice, which is, you purchase based on taste preferences. Personally, I just use wine scores as sort of a benchmark, a part of my final wine decision, but it is not the only reason for me to choose a wine.

Right and Wrong

I think part of the fear Americans have with wine is that they will choose the wrong wine and embarrass themselves. At that important moment, say a business dinner or choosing wines for a social gathering, they will choose a wine that is inappropriate for the occasion. Pairing food and wine seems to be an especially stressful decision for many wine newbies; this is my biggest request at wine classes for advice. Ordering wine in a fine dining restaurant fills the purchaser with a form of paranoia that approximates losing footing during mountain climbing on a particularly high precipice; make a mistake and you're in a free fall! I repeat often that a good wine is a wine you like, but that doesn't always satisfy many Americans' deep need for the "right" answer, the best solution and approach for a very awkward moment. Well, as they say, if you don't know where you're going, all roads will lead you there!

It's Booze

When it comes to regulation, alcoholic beverages are controlled, taxed, and restricted in so many ways that it seems amazing we are even allowed to drink wine!

Prohibition not only destroyed the American wine industry, it also made "alcohol" the goal of drinking. Why would you drink 13 percent alcohol wine when you could get 40 percent alcohol gin?

When I was growing up, if you could get your hands on some booze—it didn't matter, beer, wine, spirits, or whatever, as long as it had alcohol in it—this was the beginning of a party. Every party in high school had a keg of beer (Molson's Golden Ale, actually!) or some other wacky stuff. The idea was to either get lucky or *lit*; it didn't change much in college either! Americans have an uneasy relationship with alcohol, because it's directly connected with overdrinking. I agree that it's something to be careful with; it's a dangerous substance, but I also agree with Thomas Jefferson who said essentially two hundred years ago that people tend to be more sober on wine and less so on beer and hard spirits. Yes, of course, drinking too much wine is dangerous, but in moderation and with food it can be a part of both an enjoyable and healthy life experience. It's too bad that so many people lump all alcoholic beverages together. In Europe, wine is sometimes even served to children. Historically, water often had bacteria in it, and the best way to make it potable was to blend wine with water and drink them together. Just so you know, when they talk about "cider" in history, they're primarily talking about the fermented type, and all ages drank that in the past. Use common sense, just don't over drink.

Catch the Bug!

America is now the number one consumer of wine in the world; we just beat out France. What's so amazing about this is about a third of Americans don't drink at all for religious or other reasons, and most wine consumers barely drink more than once a week. We have lots of room for growth!

Americans pick up new things very quickly—and with the wine bug, it seems that drinking wine is more than a trend; it's become part of the upscale American lifestyle. I think the three big influences on this phenomenon are the Paris Tasting of 1976, the French paradox introduced on *60 Minutes* in 1991, and, of course, the movie *Sideways*, but I think wine consumption is inevitable in our country. My simple explanation is, if you travel and enjoy good food, wine becomes a natural part of your lifestyle. The Italian trinity is "wine, bread, and olive oil." I think the American trinity is "travel, food, and wine." Sure, many of us remember the cheesy wine marketing in the '80s around wine coolers (remember the Bartles and Jaymes guys?), but times have changed, and permanently for the better. One of the amazing thing about Americans is how we seem to accept change in some elements of our lives while rejecting changes that we deem "culturally" important. The classic example is how many Americans accept the fact that the cork is a faulty solution to preserving wine, but they can't quite accept screw tops in many cases, but prefer a plastic cork which still represents a highly esteemed closure. Screw tops represent a "cheap" alternative and although they're technologically better than both regular cork and plastic corks in many ways, Americans like the idea of a cork-style closure.

American Wineries

Now that Americans have more wealth and have traveled and experienced wine, they're creating the big boom in U.S. wineries. Many people are leaving their traditional white-collar careers to start their own vineyards with hopes and dreams of living a more relaxed, possibly bucolic, lifestyle. Although owning a winery is a very labor-intensive job, there are many retirees who are starting wineries or purchasing existing ones. Owning a winery is a dream for many who want to get back to nature or who enjoy the wine country lifestyle. Many wineries have tasting rooms and event facilities for both private functions and public events. Many weddings are held at wineries because of the romantic setting and the chance to entertain with great food and wine. The wine lifestyle is very attractive to a multitude of Americans, and many younger people are going back to the farm to learn winemaking. Many people find the wine lifestyle satisfying both intellectually and spiritually and a return to our natural roots.

Teaching Style—Express Yourself!

Teaching Approach

Before we even get started, I want you to understand something clearly—you will not walk out of this class an expert, I guarantee that.

The dilemma of teaching an introduction to wine class to wine newbies is that my attendees all have different hopes and expectations of what they would like to accomplish. Clearing up misconceptions is important, but attaining wine expertise in a short time, much less a two-hour class, isn't possible. People in *Wine Basics 101* come from all walks of life in the class: different ages, backgrounds, and experiences. Many of them have already begun to drink wine on a regular basis and have begun to form their own opinions, no matter how ill conceived. My job is to create a consistent point of view that anyone can understand and use on a regular basis in their attempts to choose a wine. How can I come up with a "one size fits all" solution that can be delivered in around two hours and satisfy the majority of my audience? The best I can hope for is that they will decide to drink wine on a regular basis and will take a few of the lessons from the class with them to jump-start their road to wine pleasure.

My Passion

I love wine and food and the world of people who make a living with their passion for it. There is nothing I enjoy more than introducing a new point of view on wine. Even something as subtle as learning to taste wine can help me realize so much more about a wine. A little knowledge can make relating to wine so much deeper. When I stick my nose into a glass of wine, I get more than just the aromas of the juice. I also get memories of past tastings and images in my mind of dishes I would love to pair with this wine. That same experience I have while tasting extends into my regular life—sometimes I'll be on a long walk, and the smell of flowers or herbs like rosemary, will bring up mental pictures of a dish like roasted leg of lamb, stuffed with goat cheese, garlic, pine nuts, and olive oil, and how that would taste so delicious with a nice Australian Shiraz or even a rustic Nero D'Avola from Sicily. Images of the Mediterranean stream past my eyes—a deep blue sea with small fishing boats all carrying the fresh local seafood, a quaint little seaside village, built right into the steep hillside, and maybe a little café serving the local wines with simply prepared, delicious cuisine. Wine isn't something to understand, it's a way of looking at the world, a refreshing perspective on how humankind can work with nature to create wonderful produce, meats, cheeses and, ultimately, turn the local grapes into mouth-smacking delicious wines! I can get poetic about wine, but frankly it's so much more enjoyable simply to sit at a table and share the experience with food and others!

Sharing

I really love engaging people in the process of learning; wine is just a tool for my chance to excite people about my passion. What I'm hoping for is audience harmony, where people are tasting wine thoughtfully, with maybe a little quiet conversation at the table, but overall a group of happy people learning about wine. It sounds easy, but most people are coming from work and, by the Thursday class, they're already tired, maybe a bit hungry, and since many don't get a bite to eat before the 7:15 p.m. start of class, a bit tensed up. I need to reach them.

UMMM!

Ummm Factor

Experiencing is right brain; information is left brain. Since wine is sensual, and the sensual side is experiential and, right brain, you need to focus on the "ummm" factor of wine.

This is hard to explain but easy to understand: when something tastes good, you get the good-all-over feeling that you enjoy the taste of something. Most people get this with comfort foods, which are laden with salt, fat, and sugar—things that wine has none of. So right off the bat, wine is missing the keys to "ummm," but it has a wonderful supporting role. It can make food taste better or bring out aspects that were not there without it. I love a good grilled steak, but it's even better with some caramelized grilled onions, salt and pepper, and even better with a big bad Cabernet Sauvignon! There's something about the combination of juicy seared steak, seared sweet onions, and the fruity, juicy, even alcoholic, combination that creates a wonderful and memorable synergy! Oysters are great, but they are even better with a squeeze of lemon on top, but even one better with a crisp, possibly stony, Sancerre or the minerality of a Loire Valley Muscadet—yumm or ummm! This is why drinking wine is such a pleasure, and it's also fun to share these experiences at wine and food festivals or just at lunch or dinner. It's like the high point of civilization to enjoy a complex beverage like wine, made of the earth, and it tastes better with great food. Life just doesn't really get much better.

I find the best way to teach people about wine and give them an enduring memory is to take them out of their comfort zone. Once I had people draw pictures with a pen of their favorite dish—it was amazing to see 150 people in a room attempting to draw lobsters and steaks!

So my approach is to push the envelope a bit and get people to think outside the box—yes, there are some simple rules and ways to pair wine and food that mostly work, but since I'm dealing with an intelligent well-educated audience, why not see how far I can get people to go? When you sit in school or at a white-collar job all day, your synapses are burned out; you've pretty much used up the left side of your brain's ability to make cognitive decisions. Why not go over to the other side and warm up your creative, artistic, experiential side, which has been ignored? Why not get just slightly buzzed so that you can "feel" wine? It's OK; it's going to happen whether you intend it to or not. Let the problems of the world go by and sit back and taste one of nature's great pleasures—this is why poetry, art, music, and other cultural events are connected with wine. I'm past all that, I just enjoy the wine and food together. That is my music—hopefully yours too!

EXERCISE 2: Think about a recent experience when you shared wine with a friend or friends—this should preferably be a memory within the last few months or weeks. Just as in Exercise 1, close your eyes and take a few minutes to imagine the people around you at the time, the wine itself, its container, and any sounds, sights, or smells you associate with the mental picture. This time, try to really concentrate on the wine or wines you were drinking at the time and on any foods you were eating as part of the moment. Really try to imagine the scene and the people: and anything that was said that made you laugh or think about the moment. Can you taste the wine and food right now in your mind? Try to make it vivid in your mind by accentuating the images, sounds, and smells. This is your "Now Wine Experience."

---

2 TASTE, TASTE, AND TASTE

Woman at an Austrian Embassy in Washington, DC, wine tasting I organized for my group, TasteDC to showcase about thirty Austrian wines: walks up to the table where I'm pouring wine. There are eight wines at the table to taste. She holds her glass very close to her body and looks at all the wines for approximately a minute, never putting her glass out to taste. She has a look of discernment on her face.

Charlie: "Would you like to try the Grüner Veltliner? This one is very good. Austria is known for this varietal!" I pick up the bottle at the ready-to-pour position.

Woman (after giving scornful face and pulling her glass away): "I'm not interested in tasting any wine, and frankly, I'm offended by your actions." (She storms away.)

Charlie in class: "OK everyone, put your nose in the glass and sniff. (Charlie isn't happy with the initial reaction and response). OK, everyone as a group, this is participatory. Everyone put your nose in the glass and let's hear a big SNIFF. (Audience loudly sniffs from glasses.)

How Wine Professional's Taste

See and Swirl

Sniff

Schlurp!

Savor - Evaluate

Heading: See, Swirl, Sniff, Sip, Savor, SPIT!

Everyone has a picture in his or her mind of the snooty wine person with the large wine glass, swirling, swishing, and sniffing the wine loudly, then thoughtfully tasting, and possibly spitting the wine out before he or she makes the glorious pronouncements. Although you could learn about wine without the professional tasting method, it's a good habit to form, because it makes your brain focus more on what's going on in the glass. It's a process, but it's not absolute. Many people have different ways of tasting a wine. This is just a way for you to evaluate wine—if you don't care, fine, but read on. I think it will improve your tasting skills and your ability to figure out what's what.

For me, the most important rule about a wine glass is it should be *big!* (Audience laughs.) I hate to look for the bottle when I need another pour; I just go right to my glass.

Step 1: The Eyes Have It

When you look at a wine, you want to make sure of two things: that it looks the way it should and there's nothing left in it. I mean a white wine should be yellowish, a red wine should be reddish or purplish, but the other reason is there might be a piece of cork in there or a bug. If there's a bug, pull him out and shake him until you get all the excess wine out of him!

As wine professionals, when we look into a glass of wine, we're primarily looking for the color and current state of the wine. Wine changes color when it ages; white wines tend to get darker colored and sometimes brown; red wines tend to lose their purply/red color and get a brick/orange color. This is just to get an idea if the wine looks vibrant or if, possibly, the wine has been overheated, overaged, or if it looks fresh and ready to drink. You learn the details only from experience; let's move on to the next step.

Step 2: Swirl, Baby, Swirl!

The best way to swirl the wine is on a table. (Charlie demonstrates by putting a glass with a little wine on a table and counter-clockwise rotates the glass with the base on the table creating a "swirl" of wine in the glass.) This is a major reason you need a wine glass—once I forgot I had a martini glass in my hand, and I swirled. The whole drink ended up on the clothes of someone standing next to me!

Swirling is the way you wake the wine up and aerate it, so that you get the maximum aromas and surface area to smell those aromas. You can do this by lifting your glass and swirling in the airspace in front of you, but it's much easier to simply rotate a glass on a table so that you don't get wine all over yourself or your neighbor. One of the benefits of swirling is that wine has been sitting in a bottle for a while and, unless you've decanted the wine by pouring it into an open container such as a pitcher, the wine doesn't really come together right away in the glass. Some wine professionals sniff the wine first, then swirl, then sniff again—it doesn't really matter. The goal is simply to get a better smell of the wine.

I get the question all the time: "What do the legs of wine tell you?" Not very much.

The "legs" of the wine are the droplets of wine that run down the side of your wine glass after swirling. Sometimes, they are thick and really noticeable, and sometimes, they are thin and run quickly down the side of the glass. So many people believe that the thick legs must mean the wine is better, while the thin legs must mean it's of lower quality—this is just not true. The legs have more to do with the viscosity of the wine, which relates to three things: sugar level, alcohol level, and possibly glycerin. The higher the sugar level in wine, the thicker the legs, so if you have a dessert wine, expect the rivulets to run heavily down the side of the glass. Since most wines are dry (the opposite of dessert wines, more on this later), it's irrelevant. Alcohol, on the other hand, is significant in that the higher the alcohol percentage in wine, the more and thicker the legs as well. This has something to do with the fact that alcohol evaporates at a different rate than water, forming "tears." Still, since higher alcohol does not mean a better wine, this is not significant relating to quality either. Finally, glycerin may or may not be in wine, but the one thing we do know is that hand cream is made from it, so let's not even go there!

Step 3: Sniff—The Noses Have It!

You can taste only four or five things: sweet, salty, sour, bitter, and "umami," which is a savory flavor, sort of like soy sauce or mushrooms. Your nose can smell thousands of aromas, and this is the important part of tasting—use your nose.

This is the most important part of actually "tasting" a wine. Since your tongue is extremely limited—think back to the last time you had a cold and your nose was stuffed; you couldn't taste very much. The nose and its sense of aroma is the key to evaluating wine. So what do I look for in the aromas of wine?

First of all, a wine should smell like some kind of fruit, because wine is made from fermented grapes. With white wines, you commonly smell aromas similar to apples or pears, while with red wines, it's more often cherries or berries. Some wines scream out peach or blackberry, but these fruits don't actually exist in the wine. In other words, there are hundreds of aroma compounds in wine, and we don't yet really know why a wine smells the way it does. The key is that wine professionals have experience and know what to expect. This may sound controversial, but I believe that 90 percent or more of sensing aromas has to do with one's experience and has a strong biological connection with survival. The reason we compare a wine to another reference point, such as fruit, is because that it is as close as we can get to understanding what we're experiencing.

Floral aromas are also primary; often I'll smell violets in certain red wines or honeysuckle in certain white wines, mint as well in many wines. There's an expression we use in wine called "high tones," which really means smells that seem to rise quickly and aggressively out of the glass, and often these are like flowers or sometimes like mint.

After fruit, the aromas go to secondary aromas, such as earth components—leaves, stones, cedar box, tobacco, licorice, etc. Again, these are not really in the wine, but they are sort of the backdrops to the fruity aromas. These are more difficult to detect when you start out because, as I mentioned before, a wine taster's experience and expectations make a huge difference. Some wines have a pronounced stinky/earthy smell, also known as "barnyard" which, depending on your take on this aroma, can either be very satisfying or a sign that the wine actually has problems or a wine "fault." French wines, particularly well-made ones, often have this aroma, and cedar box and pencil shavings often jump out of Bordeaux wines; wet leaves (or forest floor) often are the aromas of red wines from Burgundy.

Finally, there are the aromas associated with the wine-making itself, such as the type of oak used and the aging of the wine. Oak can hit your nose early in your sniff of the wine, and much of what oak smells like has to do with the type, especially French vs. American, as well as how the oak was treated or "toasted." Before a wine is put in oak barrels for aging, the oak has to be conditioned by charring the interior, actually using fire to burn and caramelize the inside of the barrel. The amount of charring, the type of oak, and whether the oak barrel has been used before, all contribute to the "oakiness" of the wine. Some wines, of course, see no oak at all, or reused oak barrels are used so that little oaky aromas occur. On the other hand, many lesser-priced wines are flavored with oak chips sort of like tea bags.

"OK, everyone try an experiment. I want you to swirl and sniff the wine (everyone does so), and now I want you to swirl, then blow air into the glass, and then sniff again (everyone does this). Did you notice that you blew out most of the aromas of the wine the second time (most people's heads nod yes)? This only goes to show you the effect the glass has—it's an "aroma chamber."

You're at a fancy fine dining establishment, you order a wine from the sommelier, and she comes back to the table, shows the bottle, presents the cork, and pours just a few splashes of wine into the bottom of your glass—why so stingy? As I like to explain it, the less wine poured into your glass, the more room for the wine to expand its aromas into. Actually, if you pour too much wine into a glass as they used to do at inexpensive Italian restaurants in those little jelly jar glasses, there is no room for the smells to emanate from. This is why I always call the space between the wine and the top of the glass the "aroma chamber." The less wine poured, the more chance for the aromas to volatize in the glass and hit your nose with their lovely fumes.

Nosey Detective

A detective looks first for clues at the scene of the crime, not five miles away. Learning to use your nose in the glass is like a detective physically at the crime scene. All other clues, such as the cork's aroma or the legs of the wine, are inaccurate. They're too far from the crime scene.

If you want to understand the nuances of wine, learn to use your nose. The evidence is literally right under your nose. You're getting direct access to all the important components of wine from fruit to wood. By the way, wine professionals actually call the aroma of wine "the nose," and they also use it as a verb as in you "nose" the wine. The secret to using your nose is to use it all the time—not just when dealing with wine, but also when you walk into a room, when you are cooking a meal or go out to eat, when you walk outside and see a local garden or a pine tree, or you go to celebrate an occasion. The secret is to pay attention—we have thousands of odors hitting our noses from morning until night, but we don't make note of them much, unless they are particularly wonderful or, more often, if they are really awful and stinky. Next time you go to purchase cheese at a store, ask for a sample of each, and before you put the cheese in your mouth, take a few seconds to allow the smells to emanate into your nose.

Serve cheap white wines extra cold—this will freeze all their aromas and stop people from recognizing the wine's lack of quality.

I always make the joke that if you have in-laws or friends that you don't particularly like coming over to your house, open a really cheap bottle of white wine that's really chilled—no one will be able to notice the difference! My experience is that I once ordered a really nice and expensive white Burgundy at a fine dining restaurant, and it was served extra cold. The only thing I noticed in the wine was almost no aromas but a very acidic/tart flavor that wasn't particularly pleasant. About fifteen minutes went by, and the wine warmed up in the glass and became beautiful and expressive with honeysuckle, apples, and almost cinnamon notes. This is why white wines should be served warmer than refrigerator temperature and red wines cooler than room temperature. In order for aromas to become gas in your glass, they need to be warmer and not totally frozen in solution. This is one of the reasons that, when ice cream flavors are made, they have to have extremely more potency than if the cream were melted; aromas freeze substantially under forty degrees Fahrenheit.

Step 4: Time to Schlurp!

(Charlie sips a little wine into his mouth and begins to suck air in, making sucking-air-in sounds. He walks over to a table, schlurps a few times, walks over to another table, schlurps, then he appears to be ready to spit out the wine into a spittoon, but he decides to swallow instead). "So why do wine professionals spit out the wine at a tasting? (He pauses to look around the audience for an answer). Well if you tasted and swallowed over fifty wines, you'd be on the floor, and that wouldn't help your reputation much!"

If you taste twenty-plus wines at one tasting, it gets more difficult as you go to differentiate what you're tasting. At some point, your mouth simply can't handle it anymore, and you get "palate fatigue." The Aussies have an answer for this; they call it "beer…ahh!" (Beer.)

To really taste the wine, you need to cover every part of your tongue and mouth—this is why wine professionals suck in air or "schlurp," as I like to call it. The purpose is twofold: to literally cover all parts of the tongue, so as to be able to maximize the taste sites on the tongue, and to agitate and aerate the wine so that the aroma molecules get sucked up for a second smell in the retronasal cavity between the tongue and nose. I always mention to attendees of the wine class that it makes a pretty funny look on your face and there is the possibility of mistakenly spitting out or dribbling wine on your neighbor, so you may want to forego this at any upcoming business dinners! On the other hand, it really increases the flavor potential of a wine in a short time so that you can choose to spit it out if necessary, as I often do at the tastings where I taste more than fifty wines.

Wine speaker: "Women taste better than men."
Attendee: "How do you know?"

So you can only taste the five flavors I mentioned before, and there is no salt in wine, so that leaves sweet, sour, bitter and the umami, or savory, taste. Some people are more sensitive to taste than others and are actually "super tasters," because they have so many sensitive taste buds in their mouths. I put more emphasis on early wine drinkers on the nose of wine, but some things stand out early in taste: wines with high acidity (some people say they're "sour") tend to make your mouth water like lemon juice. Acidity is an important component in food dishes as well, so high-acidity wines tend to taste better with food, but not always so great on their own.

In the wine business, there's a saying,
"People talk dry, but drink sweet."

I think when people start out in wine, they want to separate themselves from the people who drink cheap, sweetened, and fortified wines (Boone's Farm, anyone?), so they feel it's necessary to focus on dry wines. Most wines today are pretty dry. Less than 1 percent of the wines you'll see in the store are sweet, but early wine drinkers often have a sweet tooth. They like a little bit of sweetness in wine. This just makes sense. In nature, ripe fruit is sweet, and under-ripe fruit is bitter or sour. Many wine producers leave a "little" extra sugar after fermentation to give their wines better *mouth-feel*, so more people will like them. On the other hand, some of the world's greatest wines are dessert wines, like Sauternes from France (Ever hear of *D'Yquem*? It often sells for hundreds of dollars for a 375ml half bottle.) and the ultra-expensive ice wines from Germany and Canada.

I often compare the bitter component in wine to the white pith in citrus fruits, like oranges and grapefruits. Most wines today don't have much of a bitter component, because this can be very unpleasant. A lot of inexpensive white wines made from over-cropped grapes have a bitter component, but most people confuse tannins in red wines with bitterness. I'll cover this more in the red wine chapter coming up. Noticeable bitterness in wine is a wine *fault*; it shouldn't be there.

The final taste is umami, which confuses people a bit because of the name. If you prefer, call it *savory*. It was originally discovered by the Japanese and relates to some of their favorite tastes: miso, soy sauce, and monosodium glutamate. Some wines have this component as well, particularly aged wines and Pinot Noir. I also think of balsamic vinegar as savory, as well as mushrooms, tomatoes, eggplant, and beef. As you can tell from the taste, the wine and food combinations of savory are varied, but it's something I think about most when I'm pairing the wine with the food.

Wine professionals love to talk about the *finish* of a wine, its length, and how it feels after you've swallowed the juice. I don't put that much importance on this.

Step 5: The Finish and Evaluation

After you swallow the wine, there are the residual flavors left in your mouth, but more than anything, the finish leaves an impression in your mind: was the wine light, and did it finish quickly, or was it a long, interesting finish that went on for a long time? This is very subjective, but generally well-made wines have a longer finish and length on the palate. Red wine tends to have a longer finish than white, and dessert wines can also have a long finish. I hear less and less from wine professionals about the importance of finish, because it's very personal and difficult to relate to a new wine drinker.

Evaluating wine is easier once you've tasted similar wines in the past and gain experience and expectations of how a wine should taste. If you've never had a Riesling before, it might just give you a floral note and a touch of sweetness, but for an experienced taster we might get aromas reminiscent of roses, violets, and maybe a touch of petrol in the nose and, on the palate, a rich coating of almost oily pine and rosemary, with a bracing acidity and a lemon-lime aid finish. Did we both just taste the same wine? Yes, but an experienced taster has prior mental notes, which influence what we're about to taste. Some tasters are very sensitized, and this can also be trained. You can learn to become a better taster. The best way to get better at evaluating wine is to attend wine tastings and learn from tasting and asking questions. There's no short cut that I know of. Even reading descriptions of a wine can be misleading. I tell new students of wine to stick their noses in their glasses and go through the tasting process; in the end this will help them understand wine the quickest.

There is a Zen to wine, as there is a Zen to everything. I'm always joking in my wine class when I think attendees need more direction. I use the old '70's *Kung Fu* TV series. In my best Asian accent, I act like the young student's teacher/mentor: "Grasshopper, you must..."

Balance

When all the components of the wine come together beautifully in your mouth, we say the wine is "balanced."

When the components of a wine are balanced, we mean that the aromas, acidity, fruit, concentrated flavors, alcohol, and finish come together harmoniously on our palates. A wine might be out of balance if there's too much alcohol; then we say it's "hot" because it burns your palate, creating a hot sensation. We might put our nose in the glass and notice that something is missing; maybe the wine is "closed," so it's not showing its true potential and bouquet. Some wines "attack" your palate beautifully with aggressive fruit, but they have a "hole" in the middle, so that they disappear for a moment from your flavor senses and then reappear as flavors in the back of your mouth. Winemakers can adjust a wine to hit different parts of your palate, so they have a say in the final wine, but also the quality of the starting grapes has a huge influence. To understand balance in the taste of wine takes time, and there are again no shortcuts. Ultimately, each person has to find the balance in the wine, just as people seek to find balance in their lives. That *is* the Zen of wine!

Grape = Varietal

Wine professionals call wine grapes "varietals." So, Chardonnay and Pinot Noir are varietals; so is Cabernet Sauvignon, Sauvignon Blanc, etc. We call them varietals to separate wine grapes from table grapes and raisins.

This is less than profound but will certainly help you with wine professionals. Wine is obviously made from grapes, but wine grapes are called varietals because they have certain characteristics that make them good for making wine. The best wines today are made from *Vitis vinifera,* more commonly known as *vinifera* varietals (Chardonnay, Merlot, and Sauvignon Blanc are examples). These vines originate from the Middle East and they ultimately were spread across Europe and the rest of the world where they make classic quality wines. You won't ever see Chardonnay or Cabernet Sauvignon in your grocery store produce section, because these are the kind of grapes that are crushed and pressed to make wine. The Concord grape, which is native to North America, makes excellent jelly, but not such great wine, so it's not considered a varietal. There are some American varietals, such as Norton and Scuppernong, that are native to our country and aren't the standards from Europe, and there are some hybrid grapes here like Seyval Blanc that make nice wines. The most important wines for you to recognize are made from *vinifera* because these are what you will most likely find in your local retail store or restaurant.

Wine Temperature

When it comes to serving-temperatures of wine, most people serve their whites too cold and their reds too warm. By the way, reds were never meant to be served at room temperature. It's cellar temperature, so next time you go down into your mansion's cellar, remember that!

I'm not the anal type, so I generally just serve my white wines colder than my reds, and I serve my reds at room temperature. Frankly, most people serve their whites right out of the refrigerator, and this is just too cold. The best suggestion I've heard is to take your white wines out of the fridge for an hour so before you serve, or get one of those wine refrigerators; they chill it down to fifty degrees or so and that's just about right. Red wine was meant to be served at cellar temperature and not at the infamous "room temperature," which may have had something to do with the fact that homes used to be cooler than they are today. You can pop reds in the fridge for about thirty minutes or so, or get an ice bucket and rest the red on top of it for thirty minutes or so. That way, it will chill down a little but not get too cold.

Wine Speak

Wine is all about pleasure and enjoyment with food. The language we use to describe it does a poor job. The English language simply can't explain sensual pleasures very well; the closest we can get is comparison.

How do you describe a steak—maybe seared on the outside, so maybe *caramelized*, but is that the same flavor as in caramelized fruit or in a caramel itself? How do you explain the juiciness inside? Is it like the juice of a piece of fruit, maybe an orange or tangerine? How about the aroma? Does it remind you of, say, a goat cheese or more like a rose? If this seems weird to you to describe something you eat, how much easier could it be to describe something you are unfamiliar with like wine? It's next to impossible—so wine writers and critics pretty much make it up. Read this review:

"A sleeper of the vintage," <this wine's> 2005 displays sweet cassis fruit intermixed with licorice, charcoal, truffles, and loamy, earthy notes. Supple tannin, explosive fruit richness, outstanding ripeness, freshness, purity, texture, and length suggest this beauty should be enjoyed during its first fifteen-plus years of life.

The first comment I have is how does the reviewer (in this case, Robert Parker, who's reviewing the 2005 D'Angludet of Bordeaux) know that the wine will age for over fifteen years? The wine is still a barrel sample and hasn't even been put into bottles to settle down yet. Licorice sounds good, charcoal not so much—do I really want a wine that tastes like charcoal? On my steak, yes I like that flavor, but in my wine...well, truffles are good, but I'm not even sure what *loamy* is; maybe that's related to the "earthy" part. And what's a "note?" The same as a "soupcon" or a "touch?" Robert Parker has one of the best palates in the business, but as with most wine reviews, poetic license is the rule, not the exception. If you taste this wine and don't get the same descriptors in your mind, take heart—you're not missing anything in the wine, make your own reviews up!

Probably the most frequent statement I get is, "I'd like to describe the nuances of wine," or related to that, the question, "What am I tasting in this wine?" Actually, I have no idea. What you're experiencing or sensing is unique to you.

I get the statement all the time: "I'd like to better describe wine or break down the various tastes of wine." My reply has been consistent since I came to TasteDC—some people have incredibly sensitive palates, and some people can describe and sense hundreds of different components of wine. Whether or not you, the wine drinker, can or cannot distinguish various "tastes" isn't that important. What is important is that you enjoy the wine, but why you enjoy it isn't that important. When I say something tastes like spearmint, you may experience another flavor, maybe peppermint. And when I say, "don't you get the tobacco note in that wine?" you may not get that; in fact, that may actually make you gag a bit. I've always argued that the people who write those fancy wine critiques you see in wine publications are often using poetic license and are just trying to sell their publication. Don't get me wrong, I know some people who are trained to have super-sensitive palates and who can tell very subtle differences between wines and can competitively distinguish really difficult nuances. My point is—"who cares?"

Taste is Personal

What you taste is what you taste. Don't let anyone tell you differently; if you like a wine, it's good.

The ability to taste is related to your experience level, especially with food. If you enjoy those moldy, stinky cheeses, then wine is right up your alley.

Why do I tell new wine drinkers not to worry about learning to break down wines and figure out what they're tasting? Because my premise at *Wine Basics 101* is that wine is a European concept. It's meant to be enjoyed with meals. Many times I've had wines that were not particularly interesting on their own but tasted fantastic with a certain food combination. I think even judging wine without a food combination is a mistake. Wine professionals should talk about what food would match with the wine. It is way too biased to say a wine is excellent, good, or bad. What is the application? When I enjoy a particularly expensive and amazing wine, I often want it to be served with something simple. The traditional red wine pairing for super great wines is simple roast beef with very little spice, maybe some relatively bland potatoes. On the other hand, if I'm enjoying Thai cuisine, say a pad Thai, well then, a crisp, inexpensive Sauvignon Blanc or a slightly sweet German Riesling can make music in your mouth. I'm a foodie and I admit it. Wine should go with food.

Like Velvet on Your Tongue

Wine can also have texture on your tongue and weight as well. As we move further into the book, you'll learn about tannin (the super, rough-textured compound primarily in red wine) and the effects of alcohol on wine. Alcohol in wine is one of the main components of its body, but I want you to discover more things about wine before I delve into too much detail. I think seeing different points about wine as you go through a progression of tasting and discovery is more beneficial than lumping everything together. Now would be a good time to open a bottle of wine and sit back and have a glass, if you haven't already. Suffice it to say, tasting wine is an art form, not a science, and over time, you'll get better at it.

The three most important things to learn about wine are taste, taste, and taste.

You can't understand wine unless you perfect your ability to taste, evaluate, and relate to wine. Very much like when you first learned to ride a bike with training wheels, over time you will no longer need the assistance and you will be able to ride freely on your own! The secret to understanding wine is you need to be relaxed and confident around both the people who serve it and the product itself. A few choice wine terms and requests can make easing into the wine world that much easier. There are no shortcuts to experience, especially with wine, because every year, a new vintage is produced, and you have to end up tasting all over again. What I find is that you begin to expect certain sensations and experiences before the wine is even out of the bottle—this has its benefits, but also some pitfalls. For example, I think most people judge a wine too dearly by its price and pedigree—even great winemakers have off years and, occasionally, you'll find a diamond in the rough where an $8 bottle of wine really shines. This is why keeping an open mind while you learn is important and will aid you in the long run.

Exercise 3: Close your eyes, and imagine yourself sitting in front of a wine glass on a table. Think about its shape, type of glass or crystal, the stem, the rim, and how the light shines on it. Now imagine a bottle of red wine next to it that is already open. Pick up the bottle of wine and pour a good amount into the glass, fill it up about a third of the way up the glass. Now take your hand and hold it carefully at the glass's stem and swirl the wine on the table so that you can "see" the wine rotating around the glass in a soft wave. Now pick up the glass, look at the wine again and bring the glass right up to your nose and sniff—it helps at this point if you actually "sniff" through your nose, even though this is just an imaginary exercise. Now put the glass back down and think about the aromas—consider the type of fruit, maybe cherries, then think a bit about the spiciness or earthiness of the wine. Since you may be new to the aromas of wine, think of a smell you would recognize in a room, say cherry or cinnamon apple pie—it doesn't matter if this is how the wine really smells, it's just the fact that you're having a sensory perception. Now pick up the glass of wine and bring it to your lips and take a sip—imagine the wine touching your tongue and giving you a pleasant taste, maybe you get a very cherry flavor or you can feel the smooth texture of the wine. Spend a few moments just appreciating the wine on your tongue and the lovely aromas in the nose of the wine. Now, put the glass back down on the table and relax for a minute or so and enjoy the pleasure throughout your body and senses. This is the "Pleasant Wine Experience"—you will think about this the next few times you sample a glass of wine.

---

3 CHEMISTRY AND CORK

Charlie is hired by a corporate event planner to organize a hundred-person client event at the New Zealand Embassy in Washington, DC, to showcase New Zealand wines and cuisine for the business outing. Various wines are being poured at five tasting tables laid out in a straight line for people to walk up and taste.

Corporate Event Planner: (walks up to Charlie and sees a wine bottle with a screw-top closure instead of a cork. She freezes in place, and her face quickly changes from calm, to stressed, then aghast!) "My God, you didn't tell me you were buying your wines from 7/11. What is this all about? You realize this could ruin the whole event. I never expected cheap screw-top wines!" (She has a look of alarm on her face.)

Charlie: "Ohh, you see, in New Zealand, most of their wines have screw tops, even the really good ones! It's a cork issue. (Charlie looks at Corporate Event Planner and realizes his words are not effectively calming her down.). These are some really great wines…I guess I'll have to explain this to your group…no worries!"

Charlie: "How can people be so enamored of an outdated technology like a cork? If you're going to be historically correct, well, go back to Roman times when they used the four-hundred-pound amphoras to store wine.

The Fermentation Formula

Sugar + Yeast

= Alcohol!

Charlie gets in front of the audience and acts out in position: "Sugar" (Charlie reaches his arms in the air and makes an invisible cube) plus "Yeast" (Charlie steps to his right to demonstrate the equation) equals "Alcohol (moves to right) plus Carbon Dioxide" (moves to right).

Sugar plus yeast equals alcohol plus CO_2. Some heat is created as well. This is the formula. I always explain this at every class by physically walking across the room and showing each component: Sugar (he forms a cube of sugar with his outstretched arms) Plus (moves to his right) Yeast (a circle waved into the air) equals (Charlie moves to right) Alcohol—Yeah! (Charlie puts his thumb up in the air and moves to the right) plus Carbon Dioxide—CO_2—a gas that disappears into the air unless you keep it in the wine, so the formula is just sugar plus yeast equals alcohol. I was never a fan of chemistry and, frankly, I hate the idea of giving formulas, but this one is really important—why? Because the world of wine is broken down by geography, but the formula remains the same. Whether you make wine in France, America, South Africa, or South America, you still have to get grapes ripe with sugar and either use wild yeast or add yeast to create the final product—alcohol (wine).

Dry vs. Sweet

What's the first thing that nobody seems to notice in the formula? I never mention if any sugar is left over on the results side of the equation, and that's for a reason. Yeast does its job until it dies.

Unless it is somehow slowed down or killed, yeast will essentially take all the sugar out of wine and make its by-products, alcohol and CO_2. Conclusion—all wines are dry, or should be dry, that is, if the yeast gets to finish its job. Oh, quick point:

When wine professionals say a wine is "dry," they're not talking about the taste. Dryness and sweetness in wine are based on the residual sugar left in the juice after fermentation. Less than I percent residual sugar is considered a "dry wine."

So all wines are dry—unless you do something to the yeast to stop it from finishing its job. Of course, wineries know how to do this, but since 99 percent of all wines sold in retail outlets are dry by this definition—why do people still ask for a dry wine?

If you ask for a dry wine when purchasing, you're really not asking for anything. You're not helping the person selling to you in any way. You've just told them nothing.

Go back to my early years in Harrisburg, Pennsylvania, with Mama Adler. We're out to dinner at a nice restaurant. The wine sommelier hands her the wine list. "Please just choose me a dry white wine by the glass." I still hear this refrain even today, but again, since the formula tells you that there shouldn't be any sugar left in the wine at all, all you're doing is asking for a glass of wine—period! All fermentation is basically the same.

In some way, sugar, whether it's from grapes as in wine or in malted barley as in beer, must be converted to alcohol. In the case of grapes, they must become sufficiently ripe to produce enough sugar to produce enough alcohol, so that the wine tastes good enough.

So, have you ever bitten into an unripe piece of fruit, say a slightly green strawberry? You'll notice when fruit is not in season, you'll often get small berries that have a white/green tinge like strawberries. Bite into the fruit and you get that bitter/sour experience that is less than pleasant. In fact, the only way to really fix it is to put some sugar on top. This is the same with grapes; when they are picked unripe or before their full ripeness, you're going to get lower sugars and that acidic flavor. Remember the formula?

Ripeness = Sugar = Alcohol

So all things being equal, vines grown in warmer and sunnier regions will have riper grapes with more sugar and, therefore, more alcohol in the final wine.

Back to the formula—since yeast turns sugar into alcohol, the more sugar, the more alcohol. So which grape has more sugar—one grown in a warm, sunny region like California, say Napa Valley, or one grown in a rainy, often cool, very northerly latitude, say somewhere in France? Go back to the strawberries. Where do you get the ripest fruits and vegetables? California, right? In the northern hemisphere, you are normally going to get riper fruit from more southern latitudes (closer to the equator), like California and Mexico. There are other factors involved, but this is an important distinction—yes, you can memorize this one: warmer regions produce riper, more sugar-filled grapes; ripeness equals sugar and, therefore, more alcohol in the final wine. Now is your chance to look at the bottle of wine you've been drinking from.

If you look at a bottle of wine, you'll notice that there is an "alcohol percentage" label. This is part of U.S. law. Wines from warmer regions like California generally will have higher alcohol percentages than wines from more northerly climes, say wines from Alsace, France, or anywhere in Germany.

So grape sugars and climate are directly related, and thus the alcohol in the wine. This affects body and taste. So how does alcohol affect taste? First, it increases the body of the wine, giving it a "weightier" mouth feel. So lesson number one on the body of wine—the higher the alcohol percentage, generally the more body the wine has. We wine professionals use a super simple body scale: light, medium, and heavy; that's it. So if a wine is low in alcohol, it is light bodied; with a little more alcohol, it is then medium bodied and, finally, if it has a pretty substantial alcohol level, the wine is heavy bodied.

"Hot" Wines

Wines that are more alcoholic also taste sweeter or what we wine professionals call "hot"—people actually think that the alcohol creates a sweet wine and this can be pleasant to sweet wine lovers, but to us professionals it tastes "hot." In other words, it conveys to your mouth a burning sensation. If you've ever had a red Zinfandel from California at 16 percent alcohol or higher, you get a combination of fruit and sweet burn that can be pleasant, but frankly can be pretty fatiguing to your palate.

Without giving you a lot of detail, you can already see that where the grapes are grown affects the sugar/ripeness level, which, in turn, affects the alcohol level, which leads to the body of the wine. Are you getting this so far?

Vintage Key

Vintage is more of a factor in cooler growing regions than in warmer ones. You'll hear over and over about great vintages and lesser vintages in, say Bordeaux, and this can cause wild price gyrations.

As mentioned earlier in the book, vintage is the year the grapes are harvested *not* fermented, or aged, or bottled—when the grapes are picked off the vines, that year is the vintage. Most people get confused about vintage when they start out and even well beyond. It never seems to be explained properly. But the distinction comes to be important and make more sense when you consider that vintage relates to that season's weather patterns in that specific region and how the grapes performed. Did they get enough sun and warmth to produce enough sugar to get enough alcohol to make a nice wine, or did bad weather and related factors screw up the vintage and most wines didn't get ripe enough grapes to develop full flavors? We sometimes say the wines tasted "flat."

Sugar Ain't Sweet

If your grapes don't get ripe enough, you'll have to add sugar to get sufficient alcohol in your wine from fermentation. It's more likely you'll see this in cooler weather regions. Some of the world's greatest wines are "chaptalized"—meaning they have sugar added.

To most wine consumers, adding sugar to a wine sounds like a sacrilege. "Oh my god, no, I would *never* drink a wine that had added sugar!" This is a refrain I hear often. But remember the formula; if you add sugar before fermentation is complete, it becomes…Alcohol! More sugar added means more alcohol, up to a point. Some of the world's most expensive and finest wines have added sugar, but it's sort of a secret you never hear about; journalists are never allowed to see the sacks of Domino sugar that are stacked in the cellar. Interestingly, it is against the law in California to add sugar to wine to increase alcohol levels, but the point is moot—California producers never need to!

Acidity vs. Alcohol

There's an inverse relationship between sugar levels and acidity.

One more key point: remember those under-ripe strawberries, how bitter/sour they taste when you bite into them, so much so it almost makes you wince? This is mostly acidity, the backbone of a wine. So one more lesson: in less ripe regions where fruit rarely ripens all the way, or it takes longer to ripen, acidity levels tend to be higher than in warmer regions. If you've ever bitten into an unripe peach, you know how hard and sour and unpleasant it is to eat. On the other hand, acidity in wine is necessary, so much so, that without it, a wine tastes—flabby (another wine professional term). *Flabby* means that you taste alcohol and fruit, but it just doesn't have, well...Zing! Here's an example you're sure to understand. Did you ever notice that chefs on the Food Network often squeeze the juice of a lemon at the end of cooking a dish? This is to wake up the acidity in a dish, an important factor. The reason acidity is so important is the same for food and wine: acidity wakes up your taste buds and gets your salivation going, and it adds verve to food. My Greek friends always squeeze a little lemon juice on a dish after it's served, this just reminds them of the Mediterranean flavors and how, on a hot day, citrus/acidity lightens a dish and adds a touch of refreshing flavor. Herbs sort of work the same way; they bring "high" notes to a dish. It's part of the secret of cooking and layering flavors, but I'll leave that to the food and wine-pairing chapter.

The formula is important, and we'll revisit it as we move into more detailed information about wine, especially when you consider stark differences from various wine regions, even when growing the same type of varietal. Right now is a good time to cover another important topic that affects everyone who enjoys wine—the cork.

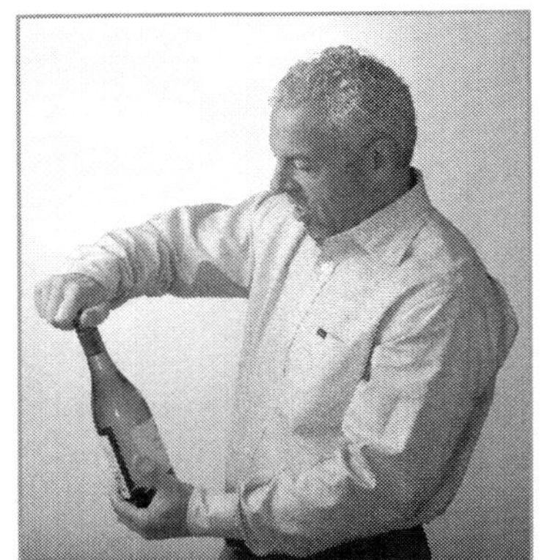
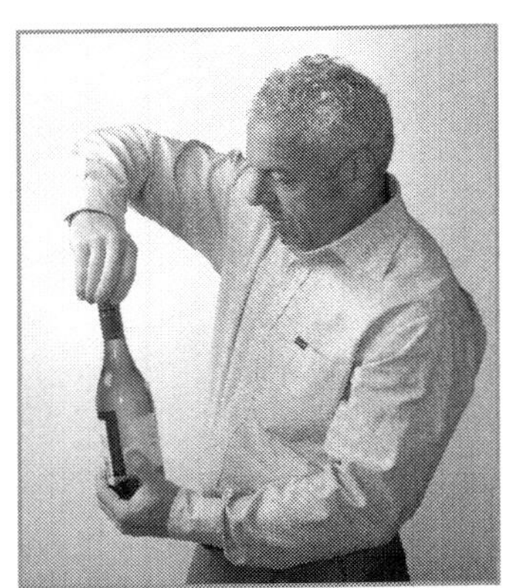
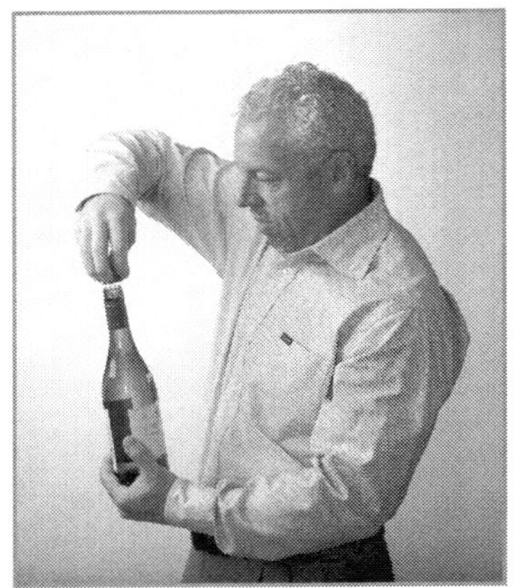

SCREW TOPS—THE FUTURE!

Screwed by Cork

The cork is simply a bad technology. If you manufactured "widgets," and one in twenty of them was faulty, how long would your customers keep purchasing them? Not long, right? And yet, in the wine industry, a 5 percent failure rate has been considered acceptable for many decades.

There is a problem with the cork in your bottle of wine—it's an outdated technology that has a high failure rate due to a bacteria found in around 5 percent of all corks placed into wine bottles called TCA (the full name is 2,4,6-trichloroanisole), which results in "corky" wines or, as we wine pros say—"it's corked!" The smell of even a slightly tainted wine reminds somebody of mildewed newspapers sitting in the basement or, sometimes, I think of wet tulip bulbs. It won't hurt you if you drink "cork tainted" wines, but they certainly aren't very good anymore, pretty much, you lose the major flavor components like the wine's fruitiness.

Cork is a natural product that is created from the bark of special trees, produced primarily in Portugal and Spain. The bark of the tree must be cured over a period of more than a year, and this is when the TCA bacteria attacks the cork. The industry has made attempts to correct the problem, but they simply don't have the technology yet and may never be able to fix the problem. Due to incredible world demand for corks for wine bottles, better cork is going to top wine producers, and inferior cork is hitting the world market for inexpensive wines. Since cork is grown from a tree, it's difficult to simply plant more trees with the scarcity of agricultural land, because the time it takes for the tree to mature is many years.

So if 5 percent of all wines are "bad" because of a faulty cork, you can return them to a store or tell the sommelier you want another wine, no problem. Unfortunately, not even one-one thousandth of the wines are being returned.

Americans have just begun to learn and understand wine over the last thirty years or so, so there are many obstacles in their way. One obstacle I think should be avoided if possible is the cork. Yes, many people are enamored of the cork. I guess it represents a quality product or possibly it's the whole ritual of pulling out a corkscrew and opening a wine. Yes, many wines of my youth that were simply rotgut had screw-top closures, and some people associate these with an inferior wine, but that's something you just need to get over. Let's face it; screw tops (also known as Stelvin closures) are a superior method for wine closure over cork. They're easy to get off the bottle, just twist off; and they're simple to get back on, just twist back on. Corks get moldy, crack, and expand when you take them out, so they're hard to get back into a bottle. Don't bother suggesting I get wine stoppers. I can never find them when I need them. Screw tops also don't "cork" the wine, and another added benefit is you don't have to store bottles of wine on their sides—the purpose of this was to keep the cork moist so it doesn't shrink. Did you ever notice how retailers often leave bottles of wine vertical—doesn't that mean a dry cork? Dry corks can let air in and also ruin the wine, another reason to avoid cork.

Then what about plastic corks? Again, this is an example of a bad technology replacing a worse technology. First of all, plastic corks are difficult to get out of the bottle with a corkscrew and even more impossible to get off the screw itself. Second, they often allow air into the wine, so they can cause oxidation, another fault.

Wine Faults

The number one wine fault is "corked" wines by far; probably 90 percent of any wine returned is due to TCA. Probably the next major fault in wines, even though I rarely see it much anymore, is oxidized wines.

An oxidized wine makes white wines browner and red wines brown/brick colored. The way I can always tell is if a white wine reminds me of a Spanish sherry, which is produced from purposeful oxidation. When a wine is aged for too long and past its prime, then it becomes oxidized. Different strokes for different folks: some people actually like oxidized wines, and the English often prefer their wines aged to the point where they no longer have much fruit. The oxidation can happen in the wine-production stage, but most often it happens with inadequate bottle storage, so this is another reason to store your bottles in a cool dark place—no, you don't need a wine cellar or a special wine storage unit. Find a dark place in the basement or a closet. Wines also sometimes get heated during transport, in the store, or in your home, and they get "cooked"—another fault that occurs around eighty degrees Fahrenheit or hotter, where the wine's flavors get cooked from heat. How can I express what a cooked wine tastes like? Not good, it has a *burnt* off-flavor that is very recognizable. By the way, the worst place to store wine is on top of the fridge; the condenser coils create heat, so you could cook your wine there.

There are other faults in wine too: for example, when you get that stinky barnyard (horse manure!) aroma in wine, that can be caused by brettanomyces, also known in wine lingo as "brett." Brett is a special type of yeast that can spoil wine, but in low doses, it actually gives character to wine. Some winemakers actually help it to occur, but it can ruin a wine at very low levels. Sometimes, wine is attacked by the same bacteria that makes vinegar and turns wine into vinegar. This is also called volatile acidity. There are other faults as well, but frankly, I don't pay too much attention to them. Wine making is so good today, that I'm seeing fewer faults in wines, except in the case of the cork—and that's unforgiveable!

Easy Access

My goal at TasteDC is to get you to consume wine with most of your meals. Screw tops are easy to open and allow easy access to wine for everyday drinking—cork just can't compete.

If you're a romantic and you feel that the cork just represents a very desirable part of drinking wine, you don't have to worry at this point—I highly doubt the top Chateaux in Bordeaux and other fine winemakers are moving to screw tops any time soon. One of the issues is how well do wines age under a screw top. Well, my opinion is, we don't really understand aging of wines very well anyway, and since most wines aren't meant to be aged very long, it's a nonissue. I've noticed over the last few years that American wine consumers are much more accepting of the screw top, and I'd say the supporters of cork are generally an older audience. I see fewer and fewer of their protests. Americans by nature love progress and change, and they seem to get the cork vs. screw top dilemma and most accept the use of better technologies. Now the question is, will people start drinking wine out of a box soon?

Keeping Wine

Probably the top question I get is how long can you keep a wine after it's been opened? My reply is always, "Don't you realize that standard wine bottles are single serving?"

I don't know if any wine preservation devices work or not because I no longer use them—I try to drink the whole bottle, and if I'm not successful, I cork it and finish it for lunch the next day! Wine loses its vibrancy of fruit flavors within hours of being opened, and it definitely changes by the next day. The Vacu-vin may work by sucking out air, but frankly, who wants to go looking around for that contraption, and I've lost more wine stoppers than I can remember, so I just push the cork back into the bottle. That is my wine-preservation system. Worst-case scenario: if you can't finish a bottle of wine, pop it in the fridge and, if you don't get back to it, say, within two days, then use it to cook with. I make some awesome red wine vinegar by simply taking old red wine and adding Bragg™ apple cider vinegar with the "mother" and letting it breathe in the wine bottle for weeks or longer. Since you can get botulism this way, you may want to experiment a bit.

Some wines keep better once they've been opened, especially fortified wines like port and dessert wines. Every once in awhile, I leave a little wine in my glass and try it the next day—you can taste different components of the wine this way.

It's fun to experiment with wine, and aging wine is more of an art than a science. So many wines today are made to be consumed young and are at their peak only a few years after their vintage. Winemakers use such tricks as micro-oxygenation, cooler fermentations, and extensive use of new oak to soften wines and make them easier drinking when they're still babies. Unfortunately, making a wine more accessible with these techniques means they often don't have enough wine components to age very well. All things being equal, drink your wines soon after opening and if you can't, make it your cooking wine on the side of the fridge.

If you're into sustainability, then box wines make sense.

Inside the Box

I don't think most people like to hear that box wines are more sustainable; I don't think many people want to go in that direction.

On the other hand, I like to get people to open up their minds to new ways of looking at wine. For so long people thought cork was a great closure even though it's pretty terrible, and many people think the more you pay for a wine, the better it is, but this is totally unproven. Why can't I push the envelope a bit and get you to envision a world of convenience: the quality box wine? The bag inside a box prevents spoilage because minimal air gets in contact with the wine, it's much lighter than bottled wine because glass is heavy, it saves on shipping costs, and it even takes up much less shelf space than traditional wine! When I mentioned all this at a tasting once, a woman seemed quite offended and proffered that there were no good wines in boxes—but time will tell. That is changing as this book is being written. I recently purchased a three-liter (equivalent to 4 standard bottles in wine volume) boxed wine produced in the Côtes du Rhône region of France for $34.00, and it was quite delicious. Considering that a standard 750 ml bottle of the wine normally sells for about $14.00 retail, I saved over $20 and saved the environment to boot! Almost forgot, recycling boxes is much better for the environment than glass too!

EXERCISE 4: Take a seat and imagine in front of you a small strawberry plant—it doesn't need to be accurate, just imagine some green leaves and a small plant. Watch the leaves grow and flowers begin to appear as the plant begins to get bushier. Soon white flowers will appear and you will see little immature green fruit begin to appear. Slowly watch as the green fruit gets larger and larger and then redder and redder until the fruit begins to swell with juice and color. Imagine picking a green early fruit and biting into it. The flavor will be bitter and sour with little sugar and make you pucker. Pick another riper strawberry and taste how the sour becomes sugary sweet. Pick an extra ripe grape that is really red and bursting with flavor and taste the incredible sweetness—notice that the sour flavor is gone. This is your "Ripe Fruit Experience."

---

4 THE SCENE—SETUP, SIDEWAYS, SULFITES, AND STUFF

From Sideways, Miles: "Thin-skinned, temperamental, ripens early."

If you smell "cat pee, cut grass, and grapefruit" in a wine glass, you're drinking Sauvignon Blanc—oh, and that's how it is supposed to smell!

Scene at Wine Basics 101 Class: The White Wine Flight

Before the start of every wine tasting, Charlie has to decide which wines to choose for the event. He always starts with an aperitif, which is normally an inexpensive sparkling wine—sparkling wine creates a festive atmosphere, and everybody seems to feel better when they have a flute of bubbly wine to sip! Charlie normally follows with four white wines, has a ten-minute intermission, and then pours four red wines into the same glasses. He thinks about all the wine classes he attended when he first started in the business and how speakers always emphasized going from lightest to heaviest wines. Another important factor is that wines should have a story or reflect a style that people will commonly see in the market and will have no problem purchasing.

The first wine in the tasting order is normally a crisp white wine that can be served nicely chilled and is unoaked. Sauvignon Blanc usually fits the bill because it is not only rather inexpensive, but there are also many different variations available from New Zealand that are consistently good quality. The Loire Valley of France also makes great Sauvignon Blanc but it won't have the varietal listed on the label, so you have to know a bit more or ask for help. A classic Loire Sauvignon Blanc is called Sancerre and is known for its minerality. Other regions to consider include Chile and California, but he almost always chooses New Zealand first because of wide availability in stores, low price, and consistent quality.

The second wine in order in the tasting is normally either a dry or off-dry (semisweet) Riesling from Alsace, France, or Germany. These are very floral and sometimes almost oily, even though they normally have a little less alcohol than the prior wine. The body in this case comes from the sugar. Riesling has a bad image among older wine drinkers, but newer consumers are open to trying new varietals. Riesling is the perfect wine for the blending of international cuisines we see in restaurants today.

There are three characteristics to this wine that come screaming out to me: the fruit, which is very citrusy (grapefruit comes to mind), the herbaceousness (think cut grass or fresh herbs) and, finally, the bracing acidity—oh, almost forgot, and that cat pee thing! (audience laughs).

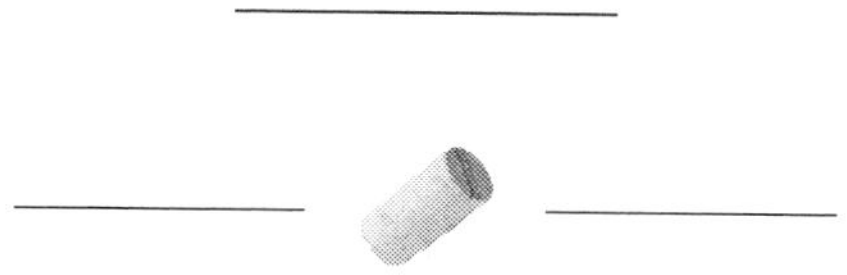

White wines were made to refresh.

Sauvignon Blanc is great to introduce to people in a class, because it is widely available and consistent in taste profile. It showcases what a white wine should be: crisp, light, and be food friendly. I rarely fuss over white wines. They are meant to refresh your mouth and make it ready for the food to come. White wine makes a great aperitif or cocktail and is perfect for hot weather. Sauvignon Blanc rarely sees oak and thus it has a light and invigorating effect, sort of like cold water thrown on you after a long hot run. It's a fantastic food wine because acidity's effect on your mouth is to make you salivate, and that's what makes food taste better, especially if you're enjoying grilled foods and vinaigrettes. The herb flavors in the wine also mean that herbs in food pair nicely, so the immediate food I think of is grilled shrimp in a lemon, garlic, thyme, olive oil marinade; a little ginger and Asian flavors would go nicely as well. The super food pairing is goat cheese and, wouldn't you know it, some of the world's greatest goat cheeses are produced in the same region where the Sauvignon Blanc is grown in the Loire Valley.

Wines that I rarely include as the first wine, but could easily replace it, are Pinot Grigio (often known as Pinot Gris, which means "gray pinot") and maybe Albarino from northwest Spain. My favorite Pinot Gris are actually from Oregon, because they can express such great fruit and floral components with a refreshing acidity. Italy is where most U.S. Pinot Grigio comes from, but much of what is passed off to the American public is insipid and derived from overproduced grapes that end up tasting like fermented lemon water. Albarino from Rías Baixas is a special wine that actually has a bit of a creamy body on the tongue and a nice combination of fruitiness and bracing acidity. It comes from a region with great seafood, and it's delicious to enjoy with various kinds of fish.

Another white wine I've always liked is Chenin Blanc, especially from the Loire Valley of France and from South Africa, where it is known as "steen." The Loire version can be a crisp and floral wine, or it can be made into a seriously rich dessert wine with residual sugar. These wines can be aged and turn into real beauties, but alas, my red wine bias and the limited selection I find in stores doesn't allow me to experiment and enjoy as much as I like—choices, choices. Other excellent white varietals you might want to try as you go are Viognier (aromas of peaches!); Torrontes from Argentina; Semillon, which is blended with Sauvignon Blanc in Bordeaux; and Chardonnay. The one white varietal you can skip and still enjoy the vast pleasures of wine is Gewurztraminer—yes, I know, I will go to hell for excluding this "noble" varietal, but it has a few negatives that I've never gotten past: it's high in alcohol, often has a bitter component, and can be difficult to pair with food. You will hear the refrain from wine aficionados that it goes great with curries and spicy cuisine, but the next wine blows it away by comparison.

Riesling for Food

Most people think Riesling is going to be a really sweet wine because that's how cheaper versions are often made. But remember the fermentation formula—all wines are dry, and that includes Riesling.

Riesling is probably the best wine for pairing with food. It's low in alcohol, has a nice acidity and, with a little sweetness, it's perfect for spicy cuisines like Thai and Indian.

I have a range of choices for wine number two of the whites, but nowadays I almost always choose either a dry or a slightly sweet ("off dry" in wine speak) Riesling, normally from Germany or Alsace, France. People often won't drink Riesling because they think it's a sweet wine, but actually a little sweetness in wine makes it excellent with spicy cuisines like Thai and Indian. Try sushi with an off-dry German Riesling, especially with the pickled ginger, and you'll probably agree this is a wonderful wine for pairing with exotic dishes. Whenever I have taught Indian and Sushi cooking classes, there has always been a slightly sweet Riesling tasted. Consistently, people in the class vote for this as their favorite wine for pairing with various spicy dishes, such as Aloo Gobi Marsala (potatoes and cauliflower sautéed with onions, tomatoes, and herbs) and Murgh Makhani (tandoori-grilled cubes of chicken in a rich tomato cream sauce). Since ginger, cumin, cayenne, and other hot peppers and spices today influence so much of cuisine, Riesling is the go-to wine for this fare.

Riesling also has an unusual quality that is pretty unique, almost an oily "petrol" aroma and texture that makes it more interesting with food. The low alcohol (German Rieslings are often under 10 percent alcohol vs. around 13 percent-plus for most wines today) means that it doesn't cause the mouth "burn" that you get when you combine hot pepper such as cayenne or habanero with alcohol. This is one of the reasons that beer is considered a better pairing partner with food than wine, but beer has one major disadvantage—it is full of carbohydrates, and it tends to fill you up faster when eating than does wine. I have experimented with literally thousands of wine and food combinations (there's a whole chapter later in the book on food and wine pairing) and, after exhausting my palate for science, I have concluded that Riesling is the go-to wine when there's spice in the food. Just so you know, the added sweetness in Riesling goes with exotic cuisine for another reason: often, there is sugar added to spicy foods to balance out flavors, a little secret that chefs have known for ages!

There is an important tension in the wine world, and Charlie wants to make sure that the class understands an important distinction: European wines are treated differently than American wines, specifically California's wines. For this to take hold, Charlie always chooses a French Chardonnay from Burgundy, France and a

California Chardonnay. These are the last two wines in the white flight served in glasses three and four. He will compare these two wines and discuss major differences in the wine world including variations in the bottle label, treatment of the grapes and use of oak, and the meaning of terroir. Sometimes the differences between these two wines are subtle, but often the California wine has a darker yellow color and stronger aroma of oak than the French Burgundy.

Chardonnay: Same Grape, Different Makeup

I want you to taste the last two wines in this flight on your own for a minute or so. Just so you know, they are both Chardonnay—even though the French one doesn't list it on the bottle.

This is my first chance to introduce the concept of "terroir" to the attendees. I always pour a French white Burgundy in glass three and a California Chardonnay in the last glass; often both wines come from the same vintage for comparison sake. After these two wines, a break is coming so that I can ask the audience questions they'd like to get the answer to and a chance for me to recollect my thoughts on what I'd like to cover in the second half. Introducing *terroir* isn't difficult to do in a two-hour class; it's virtually impossible. I want to explain the philosophy and concept of "place" in wine in ten minutes or less. Rather than delve too deeply into the topic, I know people enjoy tasting and comparing wines, so I have a little fun!

WINE LABELS CAN BE CONFUSING!

Wine Labels

So, can anyone tell the difference between the two wines? (Some people seem sure, but most of the class stares into space a bit confused.) I've just told you they're both Chardonnay, but the French label doesn't tell you that; the California one actually has it on the label. In France, they don't drink Chardonnay. They drink Burgundy; it's the region they're thinking of.

A big difference between French and California wines are that the French traditionally don't tell you what varietal is in the bottle. In this case, you just have to know that a white wine from Burgundy is 100 percent Chardonnay—by law.

When you first start out, French wine labels are very confusing because they don't list the varietal. Since the French have such a high reputation for quality, Americans often just purchase a French wine that looks like it has a nice label of a chateau or something else prestigious (unless they're novelty seekers, then it's an animal or a bicycle or something else cute!) at a price point they feel comfortable paying. The reason I'm pretty confident of this fact, is almost everyone in the class seems dumbfounded by the fact that only two grapes are allowed in Burgundy: the only white is Chardonnay and the only red is Pinot Noir, and no blending is allowed in this region. This is part of the Appellation d'Origine Contrôlée (also known as the AOC), the French way of guaranteeing both quality and authenticity of wine as well as many food products. So does the 100 percent Chardonnay from Burgundy taste different than the Chardonnay from California? Well, now there's another distinction:

In California, if it says Chardonnay or Cabernet Sauvignon or, for that matter, any varietal is labeled, it only has to be 75 percent or more of that varietal it can be up to 25 percent of other varietals.

So we know that the French Burgundy is 100 percent Chardonnay; it's the law in that region, but we don't know if the California Chardonnay is 100 percent of that varietal, at least not from the label. Many people at this point want to draw a conclusion; possibly this means that the French wine is "better" because it's never blended, or maybe the California one is better. No conclusion can be drawn yet; the class needs to refocus on tasting the wines.

The reason I chose these two wines was to make a point before the break: you can't really tell if a wine is good or bad until you taste it. There are cultural and wine-making differences between Europe and particularly California and the United States in general, but still you need to use your nose and all of your senses.

Normally, when I choose the California Chardonnay, I try to choose a wine that is readily available in the marketplace and has a strong emphasis on oak. I want the oak aromas to waft right out of the glass and hit the attendees smack in the face like smoke from a fire so there's no question of its use. The French wine, on the other hand, uses less toasty oak and doesn't normally give off as much of that aroma.

Oaky Wine

Does anyone notice that the color of the California wine is a bit darker and has more of an aroma of oak? (Most people nod at this point.) Interestingly enough, California wine making tends to use more new French oak than French winemakers do.

This is one of the ironies of wine: the French and Italians have been producing wine for a long time and have vast experience, both with their microclimates to produce ripe grapes and with dealing with the issues of creating delicious wines. California, on the other hand, has to learn and catch up quickly, but the shortest distance between two points is simply to copy. Therefore, Californians and many other newer wine-producing regions purchase new French oak barrels from French cooperages and age their fermented juice in them. In this way, they can't exactly copy the French know-how, but they can give their wines the "taste" of French barrels. Many California and New World producers do this to create consistent style wine that is very easy for the new wine drinker to taste and relate to—wines that have a definite sweet, smoky, and vanillin character derived from wood. It's sort of like when a little girl puts on too much makeup and rubs lipstick all over her lips in order to seem like an adult female. We get the message from these kinds of wines because they make a strong statement—we use oak. The tradition of French wines is to let the oak be in the background. They don't have to exploit that flavor and aroma, because...they're French!

Going Through Life—Sideways

Did everyone see the movie *Sideways*? (The majority of hands go up in the class.) "Never take wine advice from a fictional movie character, who is recently divorced and on antidepressants on a crazy one-week journey in California wine country, with his adulterous school chum." (Audience laughs.)

The one movie that has done more for wine than all others combined is undoubtedly *Sideways*. Interestingly, after the movie was a hit, a much younger crowd started to come to the *Wine Basics 101* class—and in droves! For almost a year after the movie became popular, my wine class easily surpassed a hundred people per class, and this was every other month. What I wonder is how this movie created the connection for people getting into wine. What was it about its off-center characters that really hit a nerve in the collective consciousness of twenty- and thirty-somethings? For years, the wine industry was afraid that the younger demographic wouldn't pick up wine. The fear was partially based on what happened in France, where many of the youth forewent wine for Coca-Cola and American-style cocktails. The U.S. wine industry thought that after-college, early-career types might rather drink their favorite college drink—beer—and skip the stodgy reputation of wine. Wine was for adults. Why would a younger generation go for it?

But this fear was misleading all along. Throughout the twelve-year history of running my TasteDC operation, I began to see clear demographic trends in DC. Now DC is an unusual city in that even we locals joke that no one is from here, that pretty much 90 percent of the people living here are from somewhere else, here for a job/career, and will be gone in a few years. DC has one of the strongest upper-income, white-collar demographics in the country; our industry is government and affiliated service providers, such as lawyers, lobbyists, and management consultants. We are the brain trust. Salaries are relatively high here, and people get paid for what's in their heads, not their brawn. DC produces regulations and paper, but there are no mills here! DC is sort of a microcosm of the white-collar world, and the fact is that more people in the United States today are graduating from college and even gaining graduate degrees and moving into high-paying jobs. After watching literally thousands of people come through our doors at TasteDC, it was easy to draw the conclusion that interest in wine has nothing to do with age; it is all about demographics and the lifestyle people desire.

The main character in *Sideways* is Miles and, even though he is relatively poorly paid, he comes from a very respected profession. He's a literature teacher in a private school. What's most noticeable about him as soon as he opens the movie is everyone realizes that he's intelligent, highly sensitive, and speaks the English language very well. He gives a scholarly air, but he is still human, as you find out quickly, when he begins getting into trouble with his buddy who is the cowboy of the two. Miles is extremely serious about wine and even gives his buddy a difficult time when he can't figure out why a white-colored wine is made from red grapes. You realize early on in the movie and throughout that this guy somehow understands wine; he's sort of like that overly sensitive person who plays violin that you know can relate to classical music.

Sideways really did a job on Merlot. Since Miles, rejected it in the movie, sales withered in the United States for a few years. Ironically, Miles' "special" wine, the 1961 Cheval Blanc, is mostly Merlot.

No one in the audience caught this one, and even afterward, I rarely heard much about it, but it is another irony of the movie. In the movie, Miles sings praise for Pinot Noir and condemns Merlot, so much so that he actually threatens his buddy that he won't stay at dinner if they serve Merlot. The Merlot issue relates more to the type of people who drank Merlot for many years in California—it was the juicy cherry wine that everyone loved, but it was made simply to be acceptable; it wasn't, as Miles would say, "transcendent." Merlot can be an awesome varietal, and some of the world's greatest wines including those from the Right Bank of Bordeaux can be totally outstanding. Many friends of mine in the wine industry confirmed that, just after the movie, Pinot Noir sales spiked and Merlot sales went a bit flat—it was even called the "Sideways effect." Ignoring this factor, all wine sales increased in all other "premium" categories. People began to purchase and consume more wine.

Wine Lifestyle

Sideways is an important movie because it helped people comfortably make the transition into the wine lifestyle. Since the movie occurred in wine country, visiting wineries became a great way for Americans to experience wine at the source. Many American wine consumers, who felt they knew about wine, had never been to a winery and tasted wines in a tasting room in the wine country. These are the kinds of experiences that affect humans deeply, not just intellectually but emotionally as well. The movement back to the vineyards has had a very positive effect on our local vineyards, particularly in Virginia where, every year, about ten new wineries open and more people go back to the earth for their subsistence. This local food movement, which has created the "locavores," sustains small cottage industries and artisanal producers of not just wine, but also cheeses, charcuterie, jams, and other agricultural finished products. Americans are making local gourmet products we can be proud of, just like the French have been doing for so many centuries.

All fifty U.S. states make wine. This is amazing and really good news for Americans. Not only does it mean that the United States has serious wine producers, but it also helps promote local food producers. Local food and local wine go hand in hand.

America is now one of the largest producers of wine in the world. Even though all fifty states produce wine in our country, it's very uneven in production; in fact, California still produces 90 percent of all domestic wines consumed in the United States. This is another reason I usually have one or two wines from California in the tasting. They are readily available in the marketplace. Many states are beginning to realize that supporting a wine industry is a great way to increase tax revenue and to give better-paying jobs than traditional agriculture. Economically, grapes made into wine are a much better value-added product than simply growing corn, soybeans, or tobacco. Wineries also add to tourism jobs as people visit the scenic wineries and hold events such as weddings and luncheons, as well as the whole entertainment associated with visiting a winery. Thankfully, most states seem to get it and are doing their best to protect local vineyards and wine producers. The benefits of supporting the industry will only help to make a happier and more knowledgeable wine consumer!

Suffering Sulfites

Many people think that when they get headaches from wine that this is caused by sulfites. If you're getting headaches primarily from red wine, this is not from sulfites but more likely from histamines.

If you are allergic to sulfites, then most likely, wine is not the first thing that would set you off. There are many more sulfites in other products than in wine, especially dried fruits, but there is no warning label on them—it's our government's bias against alcohol; they just feel they need to scare you a bit. Also, the reaction to sulfite allergy is not a headache, but more like sneezing fits. White wines tend to have more sulfites than red wines, and most sulfites are found in commercial white wines, particularly those in large format bottles. Sulfites are produced naturally, during the fermentation process, but more are added during the pressing and fermentation stages to protect the grapes from bacteria and are ultimately added to the bottle of wine to preserve the wine's fruit characteristics.

It's false that European wines generally contain no sulfites or less of them. This fallacy seems to return to our shores after one of you visits a quaint little café in France or Italy.

The story goes something like this: "I visited this little café in this quaint little seaside town in Italy and I really enjoyed the wines like never before, especially the reds. The server came over and explained to me that Italian wines won't give you headaches because they don't add sulfites as they do everywhere else." This story is a classic case of Americans will believe anything if the setting is romantic enough and the person talking to them has a sexy accent! The truth is that, generally, Europeans consume the same bottle of wine we Americans consume, but there is one major difference: the bottling line for the wine changes the labels for American export, and the "added sulfites" warning is required to ship the wine to our shores. Same bottle of wine and thus the same amount of sulfites, but we get a different warning label.

"So, vote on which wine you prefer: the California or the French Chardonnay (hands are normally raised about equally for both wines). But at least now you know, there are differences; sometimes you can taste them and sometimes you can't, but a little background gives you the bigger picture of what's going on in the wine world."

Now the class is a bit confused, because they've had to make a decision between two different styles of wine. Often, the differences are subtle, because French Burgundy sometimes uses new oak as well. Generally, the Burgundy has slightly lower alcohol levels, but again, they can use sugar to increase the final percentage. Normally, the California wine has a bit darker color, but it isn't always easy to discern. This is a the perfect time for a break for the attendees so they can absorb a bit of what they've just learned and possibly revive for the second half of the class, which focuses on red wines.

"OK, everyone, we're at the halfway point. Please drink or dump out at any white wines left in your glass into the empty pitchers, and we will come around and pour the red wines in the same glasses. You have about ten minutes or so to head for the bathrooms; we'll be ready in a few minutes. You don't need to rinse the wine glasses with water, so don't bother. I'll walk around the room and take any questions you have for the second half."

It's usually about 8:20 or so when Charlie finishes his first half discussion and tasting. At this point, he realizes people are tired after a long day at the office, but Charlie's work is still cut out for him—he has to cover red wine, terroir, style comparisons, food and wine pairing, and the rest of the world of wine after the break; maybe he has one hour. Charlie walks around the room asking if anyone has questions, noting what people are interested in. It's surprisingly consistent from class to class even over a decade: questions like, how long should I age a wine? Will you cover organic wines? What's the best way to store wine? Will you talk about dessert wines? These are the most likely questions, but everyone seems pretty enthused for the second half. Now, we cover red wine.

Exercise 5: Imagine yourself walking through a vineyard. If you've visited vineyards in the past, use any visual imagery in your mind, otherwise, just imagine walking down the rows and rows of vines. As you walk, think about the sounds of nature like birds singing and crickets chirping. Feel the sun warming your body and giving you positive sensations. Now you'll see a large bunch of red grapes: pick an especially ripe red grape from the vine and pop it into your mouth. Feel the sweet and sour sensation of the juice, even let a little squirt out onto your shirt; it's OK, you're in wine country! Feel the slight crunch of the seeds on your teeth, but spit them out before they get too bitter. Take another grape and more carefully bite through the skin being careful not to crush the seeds at all. This time feel the rough texture of the skin on your tongue, even roll it around a bit and get the sensations. Let the sweet, sour, and bitter sensations languish on your tongue and senses for a few moments. This is your "Wine Grape Sensation."

---

5. RED WINE—OR WHY SOME PEOPLE MACERATE EVERY DAY

Charlie is attending a wine tasting at the French Embassy in Washington, DC, in 2005.

Attendee: "So, what do you do for a living?"

Charlie: "I'm a wine professional. I run TasteDC."

Attendee: "So what's your favorite wine?"

Charlie: "Well, since we're at the French Embassy, I can tell you that the French do a wonderful job of making some really great wines. And since over half of the events I do are around food, I especially like this Sancerre with oysters. Do you like this wine?"

Attendee: "Uhh, yeah, sure," attendee says and moves onto a conversation with someone else.

I have a confession to make.
Ninety-five percent of the wines I drink are red.
Oh, yes, I enjoy a white wine every once in a
while as an aperitif or if it's hot outside, or maybe
at a wine dinner when it goes with one of the
courses, but I drink mostly red wine. It just has more flavor!

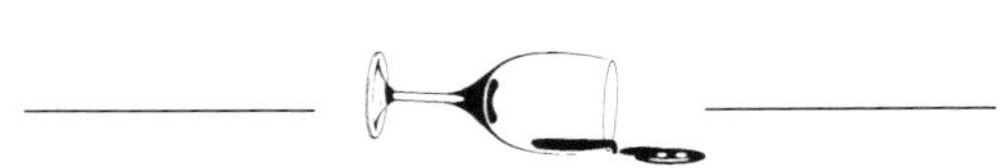

from the movie *Sideways*:

Jack: Man! That's tasty!

Miles Raymond: That's 100 percent Pinot Noir. Single vineyard. They don't even make it any more.

Jack: Pinot Noir?

Miles Raymond: Mmm-hmm.

Jack: Then how come it's white?

Miles Raymond: [laughs] Oh, Jesus. Don't ask questions like that up in wine country. They'll think you're some kind of dumbshit, OK?

Body

Volunteers from the tasting get up and go to the red wine table as they pour the next four wines in the red flight. After the wines are poured, Charlie covers the world of red wine. He begins with the differences between red and white wine, specifically tannin. He knows that many people are confused about red wine and how it's produced and why it tastes so different than white wine. The first two red wines in the tasting flight are light-bodied or medium-bodied styles that are food-friendly. He normally showcases a Sangiovese varietal from Chianti, Italy and a Spanish Tempranillo. Both wines are readily available in the local marketplace and are great wine values. Another choice is Pinot Noir which is a very low tannin wine, but it is often very pricey for new wine consumers.

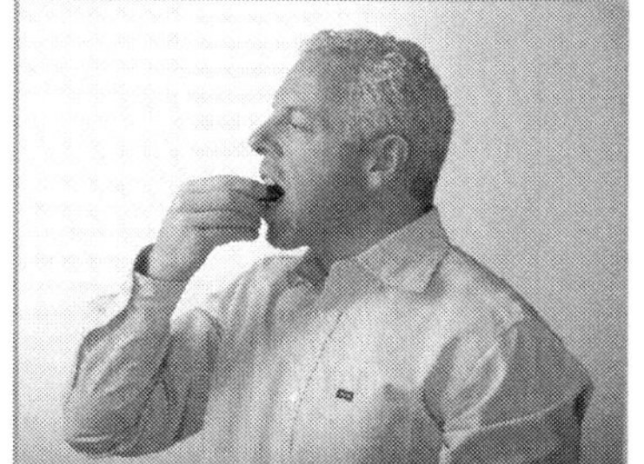

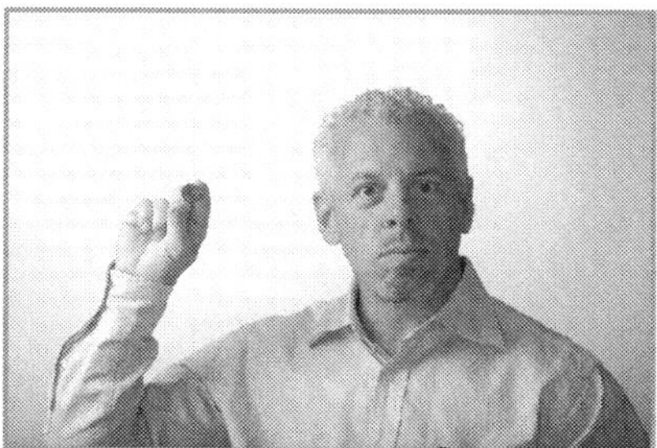

An "Ah Ha!" Moment with red grapes

You have to do more than crush red grapes to make red wine. (He looks into the audience for a red grape on a table and takes one from a table.) So, what color is the inside of a red grape? (At this point he bites into a red grape and splits it in half to show the interior. He pans the grape for everyone to see.) White! So red grapes make white wine; that's right, you get white wine from red grapes! So how do we get red wine?

My Confession

I love red wine so much more than white wine; red just seems to have more flavor. I've been told that there are actually some natural chemicals in red wine that give you a slight state of euphoria, and, when it comes to falling asleep, a few glasses of red with lunch puts me out for that enjoyable three o'clock nap I take every day! There's a lot of confusion about red wine, so I'm focusing on what makes it unique and how it plays a role in everyday wine drinking. When I was growing up, most red wines were so bad, you could barely swallow them, but now countries from all over the world produce some seriously good versions.

CHARLIE IMITATING THE INFAMOUS *I LOVE LUCY* GRAPE CRUSHING EPISODE

The Skins Have It

When red wine is produced, there is actually a separate process during fermentation where they have to extract the skin compounds and pigments to get both the color and the flavors from the skins. This is called *maceration*; basically, you soak the grape skins in their own juice to extract the flavor compounds. I mentioned in the original fermentation formula that some heat is thrown off when the yeast eats the sugar, and this heat also helps to extract more flavors as well. Often, winemakers "punch the cap" or, in other words, the skins float to the top of the fermentation vessel and form a "cap," which can be pushed back down into the juice to cause more extraction. Also, wine can be simply pumped over this cap; that's normally a slightly less aggressive way to pull out the skin's essence.

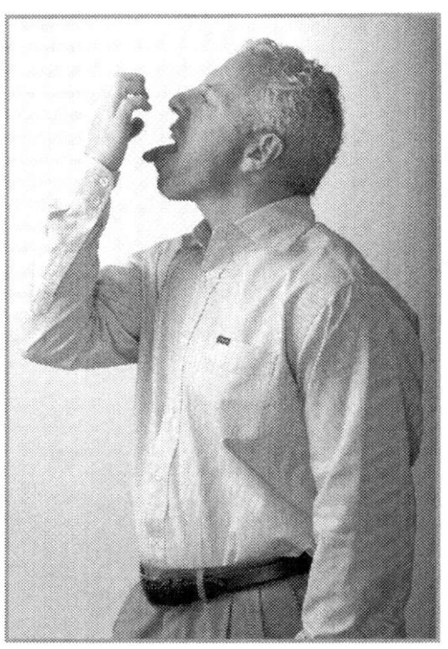

Scratchy Tannins

One compound you've probably heard about is tannin. That's what makes red wines so different from whites. The tannin in wine is pretty much the same as that in tea, coffee, chocolate, and even broccoli. It's an astringent compound that makes your tongue feel rough, almost bitter.

Tannin is the astringent compound that people notice when they first drink red wine. It's just like black tea or coffee; it has a bitter effect on your mouth, because tannins are compounds that literally scratch the surface of your tongue. Tannin is one of two hundred or so flavors in red wine, and recent medical studies have pretty conclusively shown that drinking red wine in moderation is actually beneficial to your health. The antioxidants come from the skins, and one compound, known as resveratrol, seems to carry most of the health benefits. Two of the diseases that red wine seems to reduce are cancer and heart disease. Of course, studies are ongoing, but I drink at least two glasses of red wine every day—for my health of course!

Tannin in red wines comes from the seeds, skins, stems, and, potentially, from oak. The way to soften tannin in your mouth is the same: use cream or milk (or, in the case of red wine, fat in some way), and tannins will seem much softer.

Most of the tannin in red wine comes from the skins, but there are also tannins in seeds (known as pips) and in stems. Sometimes, winemakers actually try to extract more tannin, and that's why sometimes they leave the stems in the press—this is known as whole berry clusters, versus removing the berries and crushing them after they're destemmed. Actually, there's a machine that most wineries have called the Crusher De-Stemmer that takes the grapes off the stems, removes the stems from the press, and then presses just the grapes. In some cases, as with grapes with less tannin such as Pinot Noir, whole berry clusters are pressed to increase some of the skin flavors in the final juice. As I always say, you can't generalize about the quality of the wine by how the wine is made; you have to trust your sense of taste.

Some grape varietals such as Cabernet Sauvignon have two traits that make them more tannic: 1) thicker grape skins, and 2) less juice in relationship to skin. This means that when you press these grapes and macerate, you'll tend to get a lot of puckering tannins, which means it will taste more intense. The secret to softening tannins in your mouth is the same with wine as it is with tea and chocolate—some type of fat will make it seem less aggressive on your palate. One of the reasons for this is that butter, cream, and various fats coat your tongue and smooth out the roughness of the scratchy tannins. Butter was the one ingredient I noticed in almost all dishes I enjoyed when I was in Bordeaux, where most of the red wines are primarily Cabernet Sauvignon. This buffered the aggressiveness of the wines and made it more enjoyable and palatable even with fish.

Just as wines are light, medium, and heavy bodied, they can be light, medium, and heavy tannined. It's difficult to measure this, but when you gain experience tasting, you can sense it on the side of your mouth and, sometimes, your teeth actually stick to your lips. Since I love red wines and tannin, the only way to really enjoy some of the more powerful examples is to enjoy them while eating rich dishes. Steak and roasts always go well, but the French even enjoy birds, particularly wild game birds roasted with rosemary or other spices, simply served with big red wines. Dark-meat animals, which suggests more fat, go best with red wines, but the secret is to always add butter, cream, or olive oil to make them taste better together. If you're a vegetarian, we're talking about rich flavors like black beans, eggplants, and mushrooms that work with red.

In 1991 *60 Minutes* reported on the "French Paradox" and red wine sales skyrocketed. If the French could stop smoking, they would probably live to be a hundred!

French Paradox

This is one of the momentous occasions in American wine-drinking culture that changed the way Americans looked at wine. In 1991, there was an exposé on the TV show *60 Minutes* that discovered that even though the French notoriously ate very high-fat foods, particularly the artery-clogging saturated fats, French rates of heart disease were relatively low, especially in comparison to Americans. The conclusion of the show from various medical reports was that something in red wine seemed to protect the French from the effects of the food they ate and actually reduced their risk of cardiovascular disease. Over the last two decades, more and more studies have confirmed this finding, and it seems that if you consume a few glasses of red wine per day, there are significant benefits. The direct effect of this report was that red wine sales in the United States, which had lagged behind white wine sales at the time, skyrocketed and, ever since then, Americans have consumed more red wine than white. This also opened up the wine industry in the United States to import and produce better red wines, which, up until that point, could be of pretty low quality in the inexpensive category.

Eat Fat, Get Healthy

The French paradox is that the French eat a diet high in saturated fat but have relatively low rates of heart disease, because they drink red wine. It's sort of like the milk campaign: Have you had your red wine today?

From the Movie, Sleeper, by Woody Allen:

(Sometime in the twenty-second century)
Dr. Melik: (listing items Miles—played by Woody Allen—had requested for breakfast) "Wheat germ, organic honey, and...Tiger's Milk."

Dr. Aragon: "Oh, yes. Those are the charmed substances that some years ago were thought to contain life-preserving properties."

Dr. Melik: "You mean there was no deep fat? No steak or cream pies or... hot fudge?"

Dr. Aragon: "Those were thought to be unhealthy...precisely the opposite of what we now know to be true."

Dr. Melik: "Incredible!"

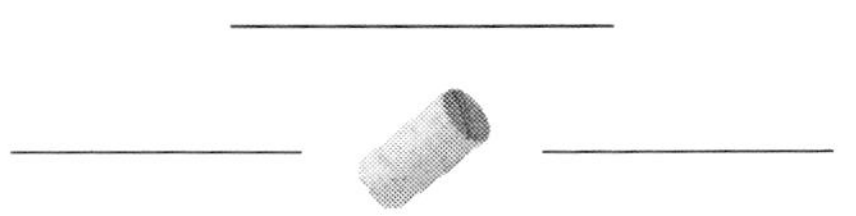

Everyone blames saturated fat and high cholesterol for heart disease in America. Many European cultures eat high-fat diets, but they eat good whole foods. I may be wrong, but if you drink red wine with your food, that's almost as good as exercise.

I love to show the *Sleeper* "hot fudge" film clip at some of TasteDC's cooking classes. I play it on my flat screen TV I bring to those events. Relating to saturated fat, cholesterol, and heart disease, I take the position at TasteDC that fat equals flavor and that all great food often uses butter, animal fat, or bacon in some combination. When I talk about American wine consumers, I'm actually talking about American food consumers, as well, because I teach classes with both food and wine. Hopping on my soapbox for a moment, Americans need to do two things better: 1) taste their food and 2) enjoy their food more. Since I believe that wine is simply a part of a meal, actually an accent to the meal, what you eat is just as important, if not more so. Whenever I ask the French, Italians, or Spanish to discuss pairing their wines with food—from tasting to tasting, where I meet Europeans—they agree that their local cuisine goes best with the wines. You rarely hear Europeans talk about foods that are "lite" with reduced fat, less sugar, or added "healthy" ingredients like omega-3 or tofu—they just don't get that. They all eat their local cheeses, eggs, meats, vegetables, and specialty dishes made with real ingredients that come from a farmer they recognize. Eat real food, drink wine, and you will be a healthier person. Relax about the nutrition of food. Real food has more stuff in it than we will ever be able to measure, and then there's the French paradox to consider: drink your red wine.

Blending can make a better wine. Some of the world's greatest wines come from Bordeaux, and the reds are a blend of five varietals.

Here are the five main varietals they use to make red wine in Bordeaux: Cabernet Sauvignon, Merlot, Cabernet Franc, Petit Verdot, and Malbec; frankly, the last one isn't used that much anymore in the blend.

The Blend

OK, there is a little memorization of varietals, but it should be pretty easy. The first two varietals are widely used and planted all over the world in many wine regions. Cabernet Sauvignon is the serious medium- to heavy-tannin wine that has very intense flavors that scream for big foods like steak and roasted foods. The top Bordeaux wines particularly from the Left Bank are normally over 50 percent of this varietal. It's a relatively rugged grape that grows better in warmer regions and can handle difficult growing conditions. It's perfect sister is Merlot, which is less tannic and often has a cherry note to it and is easier on your taste buds and smoother on the palate because of its softer tannins. The two together are an excellent match because they balance each other in a blend.

Cabernet Franc, on the other hand, plays more of a backup role in Bordeaux's great wines, because it gives the tannin and flavor backbone of spice and pepper that makes you take a second sip of the wine. Some areas of the world make 100 percent Cabernet Franc, like the Loire Valley in France, California, and Virginia where it has really come into its own. Petit Verdot is a very dark, powerful addition to the wine, so it's rarely more than a few percent. Malbec has almost been forgotten in Bordeaux, but go to Argentina and it seems to grow really well there and makes great wines—for well under $15 a bottle!

Winemaker's Art

Blending is a very effective way for the winemaker to blend different lots of grapes to create a tasty blend of wine. In Bordeaux, many of the chateaux choose their best varietals for their first label wines and lesser quality for second and even third labels. The advantage of blending different varietals together is that better-performing vines will get a higher percentage of the final wine blend while grapes that ripened poorly or had other issues can be used for a different wine or sold. Not all grapes ripen evenly from year to year. Sometimes crops are devastated by hail and other natural and created disasters which force the winemaker to literally pick and choose the best fruit for the final blend. As mentioned earlier, French AOC vineyards don't have to mention the percentage of each varietal on the label and they rarely do; on the other hand, many California wineries will spell out the exact makeup of the blend.

Definition: cépage [say-PAHZH] French for a blend of grape varieties. The "cépage" for Bordeaux reds would be the percentage of each varietal blended into the final juice.

A Little Champagne

There are only three varietals allowed to make Champagne, and two of them are red.

Even though you don't think of Champagne as a red wine, only three grapes are allowed to produce it: Chardonnay, Pinot Noir, and Pinot Meunier—the last two are red grapes. On a side note, the French often call their red grapes black as in "noir." The skins often get so dark, they are considered to be black. Even with these dark red skins, you can still make white or rosé-colored wines. Remember how I talked about the color of juice inside a red grape? All you have to do is "bleed off" the white juice before it's spent much time in contact with the red skins during maceration. If you give it a little time, say a few hours' skin contact, you'll get a pink wine called rosé; less time and you get a virtually white wine. In Champagne, they actually will mention on the bottle if it's made from Chardonnay only; it would say "Blanc de Blanc," which means "white from white grapes"; if it's made from either of the red grape varieties, it will say "Blanc de Noir," meaning "white from black grapes." These same labels are used in other wine regions for sparkling wines even when different varietals are used—everybody loves to copy the French!

Rosé has a really bad reputation in the United States because it used to be that all pink wines were made sweet. In the last few years, I've noticed how wine consumers have picked up on the fact that most rosés are now dry, and they are great wines to enjoy on a picnic.

Going Pink

For a long time, American rosés were made pink and had a lot of sugar in them because many consumers enjoyed sweet wines—even of poor quality. The French enjoy rosé traditionally as a wine to be served chilled, and it's dry as a bone with usually a light strawberry and floral flavor with bracing acidity so that it matches beautifully with charcuterie, cheeses, and basic picnic salads. The short story on French rosé is that it's a classic story of the smart French farmer. Since red wines often need to age in barrels for months and sometimes over a year to mellow and gain flavor, the farmer needs to make some income while waiting. The strategy is to "bleed off" or take some of the early juice after fermentation, before it really spends much time with the skins, and sell it immediately as a crisp wine with just a touch of the red wine flavor. The added benefit is not only immediate cash flow but, because the juice is "bled" off the rest of the red wine, this intensifies what's left, making the red wines even more powerful and delicious. Remember—wine making and agriculture is a business; the farmer has to feed his or her family somehow.

EXERCISE 6: This time you are going to do a simple physical experiment. Go out and purchase some tea bags of preferably a black or dark tea and a small container of heavy cream. Get two tea cups/mugs and put a single tea bag in one cup and two tea bags in the other tea cup. Add almost boiling water in each cup, let steep in the one-tea-bag cup for about three minutes and a few minutes longer for the two-bag cup before removing both tea bags. First taste the single-tea-bag cup of tea and get a sense for the astringency and rough texture on your tongue. Drink a little water and take about a one minute break, and then taste the two-tea-bag tea and get a sense of the same roughness and texture on your tongue. Put about one or two teaspoons of cream in each tea cup and stir thoroughly into the teas and taste the two teas again. You should notice that the cream "softens" the astringency—the same chemical tannins that give red wine astringency. Just as in tea, fat softens the red tannins in wine. This is your "Tannin Sensation."

---

6. CALIFORNIA VS. FRANCE: OR PAMELA ANDERSON VS. AUDREY HEPBURN

Early in my wine-drinking (tasting) career in 1998, I took the train to some wine functions in New York City, and on a particularly empty morning train, I noticed a woman seated with about five wine and food "lifestyle" magazines, so I asked if it was OK for me to sit next to her, and she agreed.

Woman on Train: "I want to plan a wine tasting for a social gathering. Of course all the wines will be French. A native French speaker at a wine dinner told me that California wines weren't any good because they grow their vines too close to the ocean. He said the salt air ruins the quality."

Me: "But France's greatest wine region, Bordeaux, is next to the ocean."

(Later on the train):

Woman on Train: "Either way, for this special wine tasting, we won't be opening any bottles of wine that cost under $30 a bottle; none of those wines are any good."

Me: "I guess, I must be drinking a lot of really bad wine!"

Charlie: Trying to understand terroir is like trying to understand what love is. No one can really tell you why or if it's happening, but you sort of feel your way through it."

The last two wines in the red tasting flight are a French Bordeaux and a California Cabernet Sauvignon or Merlot. Charlie wants to dig deep into the obvious differences between French and American treatments of wine. He'll discuss the influences of terroir on wine and how the professional wine world is divided about the importance of natural wine making vs. the use of technology. There are many topics to cover including the globalization in the wine world, the power of wine critics and wine scores, and the change in wine styles. Charlie knows these are difficult topics, but he realizes that new wine consumers often get annoyed and confused about subtle distinctions between wines.

Two wine regions exemplify two totally distinct wine styles that reflect the world of wine: France vs. California. The reason I use California vs. the United States as a whole to compare is primarily because ninety percent of all domestic wines in the United States are produced in California, and the stylistic differences become more pronounced if we include only this one state. The themes I cover vary from class to class, but normally I try to show that not only can you taste the difference, but you can understand it too, and how it affects other wine regions throughout the world.

Pamela vs. Audrey

I like to compare French wines to California wines as two totally different styles. Can you picture the difference between two famous women, Audrey Hepburn and Pamela Anderson?

This comparison always gets a laugh at *Wine Basics 101*. It's a not-so-subtle comparison of two women who seem to exemplify two totally different "stylistic" points of view. This is very similar to the dichotomy in the wine world. I use the visual reference because, no matter what can or cannot be said about these two women, you would never mistake one for the other in an elevator, the difference is so stark. It's Audrey (France) vs. Pamela (California): elegant vs. over-the-top, classic vs. modern, subtle vs. blatant, nuanced vs. powerful, natural vs. technological, feminine vs. sexy, and understated vs. opulent—these are adjectives actually used by wine critics to define these wines! These differences between the philosophies of France and California correlate pretty closely with how their wines are produced and, ultimately, how they taste. France represents tradition: they've been producing wine for many centuries and they understand how different sites can lend different qualities to the final wine; they understand their terroir. California, on the other hand, is newer to the world of wine production, having only seriously produced great wines since the early twentieth century, so they're still trying to figure out exactly what they have.

Tradition vs. Technology

France is about tradition, and California is about technology and innovation. Not only are the climates totally different, but the philosophies are often opposites: in France they know what they have; in California they're still learning. French laws are strict about what is and what is not allowed in the vineyard; American laws allow room for experimentation.

One detail about French wine and European wine in general is that there are often very strict laws about what can and can't be grown in given designated "appellations." In France, the AOC system controls everything from the winemaker's choice of grapes, to when they can be picked, minimum alcohol levels, and other restrictions. Wine, like food, is controlled by these laws. For example, Roquefort cheese is controlled by the AOC system. The AOC does not just enforce the rules, it is also a quality control system that guarantees "authentic" products. When you taste a French Burgundy, you do not really taste Pinot Noir; if you're drinking a red wine, you are tasting the place, Burgundy. As you know, Champagne is a region, as is Bordeaux, Loire, Alsace, and the Rhone. Each of these has AOC controls that ensure wines that speak of the place. Each region grows a different mix of varietals based on history, experience, and what will ripen properly. Cooler regions generally grow grapes that ripen early or do very well in cooler weather; warmer regions tend to grow heartier grapes that can stand the heat of summer and can produce sufficient acidities. Not all wines from these regions are controlled by the AOC, but you do know if you see their label on the wine, you're going to get a wine that is "true" to its place.

California has been producing serious wine only since the early part of the twentieth century. If we ignore the contribution of early Spanish settlers and even the nineteenth-century wine boom, they are relatively new to the wine world, but growing quickly. California's wine evolution began with producing inexpensive and often sweet wines, particularly for the jug wine market, and often they would even use French protected names like "Burgundy" and "Chablis" on these large bottles of inexpensive juice. From early on, California has imitated the French in their wine-making style: use of French oak; choosing popular French varietals, like Chardonnay and Merlot; using French techniques, like stirring the lees (dead yeast cells that settle at the bottom of barrels); aging in oak and other methods to create wines that are similar to those of the French. As they say, imitation is the sincerest form of flattery. You will see in marketing materials and hear from California winemakers how they use French techniques.

The key difference is that the appellation system in the United States is much less restrictive and has more to do with labeling the wines properly. You can grow Pinot Noir and Chardonnay anywhere in California, but in France, the AOC restricts what regions can and cannot grow them and how they grow them. The spirit of the West exists in California, where you can purchase farmland and turn it into a vineyard with your choice of varietals. France knows their terroir. California is still learning.

"Terroir" = "Character"

Definition: Terroir—(from www.terroir-france.com). A terroir is a group of vineyards (or even vines) from the same region, belonging to a specific appellation, and sharing the same type of soil, weather conditions, grapes, and wine-making savoir-faire, which contribute to give their specific personalities to the wine.

Terroir is very hard to explain to an American. The simplest way to explain it is to say that it is the microclimate, soils, geography, and things surrounding a vine that make it produce grapes of a certain quality. Another word that comes to mind is "character." Terroir is the character of the grapes.

Europe has seen wars, pestilence, famine, and many calamities over the last couple of thousand years. When you want to know about character, all you have to do is walk into a French village and see buildings that are hundreds of years old, possibly built by the Church or a monastery many centuries ago, and sometimes you'll even see bullet holes from various wars. This is what I mean by the concept of "character." The character of a wine is so much more than just where the grapes are grown; it is also the history of the village and its people and how this relates to producing wine. The French have a long history of struggles, and this builds human character as well as grape character. So when a Frenchman talks about "character," he's really telling you that people have terroir too.

The French often say that the "vine must suffer" in order to maximize the flavor potential of the grapes. It's sort of like watching one of those classic black-and-white French movies. Can you picture the mysterious man sitting at the café with his newspaper, taking big puffs off his cigarette (Charlie copies him in his best French accent), "Ahh, yes, the vines must *sufferrr*."

I often kid about the French culture in my class because I think Americans have a love/hate relationship with the French overall. On one hand, they're known to be a difficult, argumentative sort and, notoriously, they disagree with the English and us on all things political. On the other hand, when it comes to culture, especially when it pertains to food and wine, they are the experts, and they have set the standards for great cuisine for over a century. We trust the French to be right about these sorts of things, because they're...French!

Zees is my best French impersonation!

But what is it about these Gallic pronouncements that we, as Americans, relate to, or disagree with? What is the crux of our cultural differences? To the French, Chardonnay is not just Chardonnay. You can't just plant the same two vines, say they are genetically the same (many vines are clones) in two similar geographic places, and expect to get the same-tasting wine. Americans translate this to mean that we can "taste" the terroir, but it's not that simple; the story behind the wine is very important, and knowing where the wine comes from does make a difference. Taste is only one component of the concept of terroir; history, geography, and the people surrounding the vineyard are just as important. You are not drinking a Chardonnay; you are drinking a village or plot of land in Burgundy that has a history behind it.

America has terroir too, but we don't always recognize that fact. Ask someone from Philadelphia, Pennsylvania, who makes the best cheesesteak, and they'll tell you a specific restaurant they like. The fact that Cheez Whiz is used in the recipe makes no difference. Now that's pride of ownership.

American Terroir

Cajun food from Louisiana, Pacific salmon from the Northwest, BBQ from North Carolina, Maine lobster, these are American terroir. These are items we are proud of. Each region has its own way of presenting its cuisine and the drink that goes with it. When I was at the IPNC (International Pinot Noir Conference) in 2006, the Oregon Pinot Noirs were served with local salmon dishes, and they were delicious together! When I say "pride of ownership," what I mean is that there is something unique and special, even about simple foods, probably even more so if they're peasant foods. I've been in more than a few arguments about who makes the best BBQ in the United States. Most of us can't even agree on what the best sauce is! In Europe, this sense of tradition and honoring the skills of generations before them is their ongoing terroir; in the United States we are still developing it.

Terroir is the "placeness" of wine, the expression of a given location and region.

I get the question all the time: "Can we actually taste the soil?" My reply is no, we probably can't taste the soil's minerals and nutrients; that's most likely a fallacy, but we can taste the final expression of place.

The Terroir of wine reflects the life cycle of the vine

THE SUN GIVES ENERGY TO THE VINE

THE ROOTS DIG FOR WATER AND NUTRIENTS

THE VINE USES ITS ENERGY TO RIPEN GRAPES

Terroir is more than just soil, weather, position of slope, and geography; it has just as much to do with the life of the vine. A vine has deep roots like a tree or bush (Charlie widens his stance, bends his knees and reaches toward the ground as he spreads his arms), and these roots search for nutrients and water. As the top of the plant searches for energy from sunlight and heat, the roots spread out from year to year. The French like to say that vines "don't like wet feet," so soil drainage, such as with rocky soils, can make a big difference.

Heard It Through the Grapevine

I've heard that the main "tap" root of a vine can go down 150 feet or more. If you let a vine grow naturally, it will climb up everything, as vines do, even up trees. Plants have a life cycle, and a vine is very similar to a human's life: during the youth cycle (it takes about three to five years for a new vine to produce fruit), the roots are not that deep, and the vine isn't developed much; it's just beginning to thrive. Over the next forty or fifty years (vines can live to be over a hundred), it develops its root system and character as it produces more and more berries, but eventually it begins to get old and produce fewer but more intense berries—sometimes these are called old vines.

There is a point when a winemaker simply decides that it's time to pull up the vine, even if the plant has more life ahead of it.

Usually, this is around forty years; after that, generally, a vine's production of quality grapes begins to dwindle significantly. Older plants tend to have thicker trunks and much less berry production, so much so that it becomes less and less economical to pick these vines. There are other ways to increase berry flavors.

The goal of a vine, as any plant, is to reproduce. The plant ripens fruit so that bugs, animals, or humans will eat the delicious sugary fruit and place the seed potentially with a little fertilizer into the soil so that the plant may start again. Sometimes plants need a little help making their baby fruit ready.

So a deer sees and smells the ripe grape, eats it, digests it, and leaves a seed in excellent manure to propagate. This kind of thing happens all the time. Many of my wine-making buddies in Virginia tell me that they know when sugars in grapes are ripe, because the deer start to eat the fruit! Nature is in balance, but sometimes the plant doesn't quite agree. A farmer's job is to get the fruit optimally ripened, but the plant also has interests in growing arms and legs to get more light. Also, vines often produce more fruit than they're capable of ripening, so sometimes, the farmer has to cut back some of the fruit. This is also known as "green harvesting."

"So, which will have more flavor—grapes from a vine that has twenty bunches of grapes, or the same plant that has only two bunches?" Charlie answers for the crowd: "The two bunch one, right? Because the plant can put all its energy and intensity into just those two bunches vs. spreading itself too thin on too many clusters."

Yield vs. Flavor

One way to get really intense compounds and flavors is to reduce the crop yield of a plant by either cutting off its arms or actually cutting grape clusters off (green harvesting). There are other things that you can do to make the plant compete for water and make it focus all of its energy on its babies to make really intensely flavored grapes: you can plant vines close together so that they struggle to place their roots to reach water. Planting close together also causes competition for light that makes the plant use up even more energy. You can also restrict water. Happy cows make milk in California, but unhappy vines make more interesting wine.

In California, most vineyards have some type of irrigation, like a drip method that drips water on top of the soil. In France, most AOC wine regions forbid any irrigation. The plant must get its water from rain or anywhere else it can find it.

In California, it is often impossible to grow grape vines without irrigation, while in France there tends to be more variation in weather patterns. California wineries can restrict and change the amount of water offered to their vines, but this is really the point—they can determine the plant's growth more closely and the resulting wine. The French are left to nature's whimsy. Sometimes they get great wine, and sometimes they have bad vintages. Today, you are starting to see more California wineries "dry farm" (not use any irrigation at all) so that they get the true expression of their local terroir. Many California and New World wineries use less human manipulation of the vine, but this depends on the type of wine. Most of the wines you see in the store under $15 a bottle from these regions see lots of new oak, sulfites, and are produced with all the chemistry modern scientists can manage on the land.

Dealing with Vintage

Vintage is more of an issue in France and other cool-weather regions.

Since French wine making rules generally don't allow irrigation, and it's difficult to fully ripen grapes in the cool northerly climate, the French have no guarantee of a good grape harvest. Unlike France, In California, most years the grapes ripen completely. Although there are other factors that can stop grapes from ripening other than cool climate (hail can destroy vineyards, so can bugs and animals, wars too!), if you take a region like Burgundy, France, maybe three years out of a decade are very good, a few years are acceptable, and maybe three years have poor ripening. When grapes don't get ripe enough, they don't have enough sugar to get alcohol levels high enough (this is correctable), but they also don't develop flavor and concentration very well. You'll hear of wines that are "reedy," which means you don't taste much fruit; instead, you get earth, stone, and other tastes that are out of balance. Since fruit should be the primary flavor of wine, it's almost impossible to fix these wines.

Cute Puppies

> Comparing California to France is like comparing a puppy to an older dog: everyone loves a cute puppy; it licks you right in the face; it's cute and easy to love; older dogs have lots of character and personality, but they take more time to appreciate.

So you might enjoy bigger, more robust style wines from California, or you may enjoy more restrained, earthier style wines from France with their higher acidities. As always, life is choices, but you don't have to choose only one. Let the wine fit your particular application. When I want to demonstrate a wine of power and lot's of jammy fruit, I think of warm-weather region wines like California Cabernets or Australian Shirazes. When I want something with more finesse that is more food friendly, I might go with slightly more subtle Bordeaux from the Left Bank or a nice Sangiovese from Italy like a Chianti Classico. I know I'm going to get loads of fruit and pretty good alcohol from the warmer-region wines, so I do think about price points. Maybe I want to spend only $20 or less per bottle. I know with "finesse" wines like French red Burgundy, I may have to pay a big premium for the smaller winemaker's efforts, so maybe I think $35 per bottle. If I'm all about saving money, then I go to South America for possibilities, maybe pick up a nice Argentinean Malbec for $12 a bottle, or a Spanish Tempranillo for about the same price. Over time, I've picked up preferences, but it's always based on my goals and the application.

When I first started learning about wine, it was called Old World style vs. New World style of wines. Old World was France, Italy, Spain, and Germany; New World was California, Australia, South America, and many new up-and-coming regions. This is the same as the France vs. California point: cooler region vs. warmer region, tradition vs. modernity, nature vs. technology, and food friendly vs. fruit forward.

Jet-Setting Winemakers

The lines were drawn pretty clearly for me when I first began taking wine classes in the '90s. There were two main styles of wine: Old World and New World, and you could taste the difference, because they were, in fact, that different. Although it may have been that way, the wine world has changed in the last ten years or so, because many winemakers now produce wine twice a year: once in their own region and then about half a year later in the opposite hemisphere. When it's spring in France, it's harvest time in New Zealand, so that a French winemaker can get twice as much experience and vice versa. New technologies and wine-making techniques have become international in scope; French winemakers learn from new technologies, and California winemakers experience French terroir. Wine today is better than ever; it's more consistent, fruit gets riper from year to year because of better wine-growing techniques and global warming, and major flaws in wines are fewer and fewer. You can get a decent wine each year even from difficult wine regions for $10 a bottle or so, and you get more consistency from year to year.

Jammy means very ripe fruit flavors, concentrated like jam. This is associated with New World wines from places like California and Australia. I like to think the juicy fruit is easy to love and appreciate; it is blatantly fruit forward and fun.

The International Style of Wine

With better wine-making technology and the ability to get fruit extremely ripe, more winemakers are creating fruit-bomb monster wines that critics love, but which often are quite overwhelming to the palate. This is the international style of wine making (also known as "Parkerization," due to the wine critic's imprint on these wines), which has been directly affected by the jet-setting winemakers exchanging notes and techniques for extracting more concentrated flavors. What you'll notice about these new "mega" wines is that there is more use of Cabernet Sauvignon and Merlot added to more traditional blends, where they had never been blended before, to make super wines. In fact, they are actually called this in the case of the Italian Super Tuscans, a richer, more alcoholic style of wine that critics adore and give big point scores to. A one-word adjective you'll often hear nowadays about wines is "jammy"—it's just that, when fruit is so concentrated in a red wine that its flavors are thick as jam. You also think of sweetness with jam, but it isn't sugar; it's simply concentrated fruit flavors in a dry wine.

Many wines are associated with the "international style" from traditional benchmark regions to New World areas including these expensive examples:

– Super Tuscans like Sassicaia and Tignanello, both very expensive;

– Garagistes wines made by small producers, who started in Bordeaux, like Jean Luc Thunevin and his famous Valandraud wine that is literally produced in the basement of his home;

– Bordeaux top growths, like Latour and Lynch-Bages, now use more modern wine-making techniques to get more extracted riper grapes for fatter wines;

– Burgundy, notoriously the holdout for "natural" wines is getting warmer vintages and more extracted fruit wines;

– California cult wines like Far Niente and Screaming Eagle, which are made in very small production but have huge demand for their wines and prices, can skyrocket into the hundreds and sometimes thousands of dollars per bottle;

– Pingus and Clos Erasmus are two examples of international wines with heightened prices due to Parker reviews; and

– Australia's Grange and other wineries that produce highly extracted and alcoholic wines, mostly Shiraz, get very high scores.

The international wine style has not only affected the most high-end expensive wines, but also wines from winemakers who want to get higher scores from the critics as well. The one-hundred-point wine scoring system used by Robert Parker and *Wine Spectator* among other wine critics, has created score inflation: more wineries want to produce wines at ninety points or above, and they use techniques, such as micro-oxygenation, severe crop reductions, new French oak, and more extracted wines that emphasize fruit over finesse, and power over nuance. For a generation of Americans brought up on Coca-Cola and soda in general, these wines seem almost sweet and satisfy the instinctual love of all things fully ripe, but they sometimes lack delicious components that actually refresh your palate. Everyone loves a chocolate milkshake, but do you want to sip that with every meal?

The Wine Critic

Charlie: Most people don't rely on a critic like a movie critic to decide for them if they're going to see a movie or not. I mean we are all comfortable choosing a movie on our own. On the other hand, when it comes to wine, we have a lot less experience, so we often rely on a critic's choice. Wine critics are so powerful that they can, in fact, make or break a winery.

The *Wine Advocate* and *Wine Spectator* are two publications where the wine critics are so powerful and influential that they can actually directly influence consumers' buying decisions and the ultimate profitability and success of a wine. The key to understanding their effect is the one-hundred-point system that both publications use, which Robert Parker originally introduced. He is the publisher and main wine critic of the *Wine Advocate* and the most influential wine writer in the world by far today. He is so influential in the wine world, particularly in Bordeaux, that his reviews and point scores can actually determine the price and demand for some of the world's finest wines. Marvin Shanken, a former investment banker, owns *Wine Spectator*, the world's number one subscription lifestyle publication. Together, these two publications and their wine critics can make or break a wine in the marketplace.

Americans love competition and the ability to objectively score a product. The "Ninety Pointers" are those people who don't feel they need to think about their wine purchases; they just rely on someone else's advice.

The one-hundred-point system rates wines based on evaluations, where fifty points is given to a wine automatically, eighty-five points to eighty-nine points is considered a good effort, ninety to ninety-five is very good, and ninety-six and above is extraordinary. The market reaction to these scores is not so subtle: many wine retailers know that certain purchasers specifically will buy wines rated only ninety or above, and those wines have their scores listed prominently. The scores are a great way to get a quick idea if the wine is rated highly, but it doesn't tell you an important fact: how it will taste with food. There might be a really great Chardonnay that scores ninety-two points and costs $40 a bottle, but if I'm having a delicious piece of light fish in olive oil, lemon juice, and garlic, I might prefer to have a crisper wine like a Verdicchio from Italy, produced in a region known for seafood.

Wine tasting is *very* subjective; in fact, the glass, the temperature of the wine, the color, what a taster has tasted before, and many factors influence the final score. Both Parker and *Wine Spectator's* critics like Big Wines—high alcohol, high extraction of fruit flavors, and concentrated skin extracts that hit you like a sledgehammer, so a delicate wine isn't going to have much of a chance. Their influence is critical to the success of a winery, and many wines today fit this "international" profile and are probably too "hot" to really enjoy with a nice plate of food. Pamela Anderson usually beats Audrey Hepburn when we score based on how "voluptuous" or "sexy" a wine is, but maybe Audrey's subtle beauty works better with your meal.

If you don't believe global warming is occurring on our planet, all you have to do is visit wineries in the north of France where, once, grapes rarely got fully ripe (like Champagne), but now they have excellent harvests almost every year.

Global Warming

Areas of the world that were once too cool to consistently grow wine varietals are now warm enough to get the grapes sugar ripe. An unusual example is the south of England, where only a very little wine was once produced, but they're now counting on better weather to significantly increase the size of their sparkling wine industry, which could potentially compete with Champagne. The direct problem of global warming is that wine regions are shifting farther from the equator, which could mean devastation for relatively warm regions in California, Italy, and Australia. Where vintage was once an issue in cooler areas like Champagne and Burgundy, in France and particularly in Germany, we're seeing wine grapes that ripen consistently from year to year and more great vintages like 2000, 2003, and 2005 in Bordeaux. The effect is very obvious on the "international style" wines in that their alcohol levels are increasing year to year, especially the 2003 wines in Europe, when an incredible heat wave actually killed thousands of people who lived in dwellings without air conditioning, and ripe sugar levels were off the charts.

Sustainable Solution

Global warming and farming's detrimental effects on nature have given the wine industry the impetus to aggressively support sustainable methods in the vineyard. Many winemakers are changing their operations to use less electricity, less water, and to overall have less impact on nature. Some examples include putting a winery on the side of a hill so that gravity-fed winemaking will naturally crush the grapes and require less energy use, use of solar power when possible, and better management of water resources. There are many ways to reduce a winery's environmental impact from growing grapes to the final bottling. Even something as simple as going from glass to plastic bottles reduces the weight of the final wine and reduces the shipping weight and ultimate use of energy per bottle. Use of cover crops, such as clover, help to prevent soil erosion; they displace other weeds, put more nitrogen into the soil so that fertilizers become unnecessary, and support good bugs that kill the bad bugs that destroy grapes and vines. Even use of natural wildlife, such as hawks and owls to prevent rodents and moles from destroying the vines is a creative and natural way to help make wine without using chemicals. Many winemakers are sensitive to helping nature, and often it is also a very effective marketing tool, as more Americans want to do their part to save the environment.

I don't necessarily prefer organic foods or wines because of their taste; the difference is probably negligible. Organic or "sustainable" practices are important to me in growing all crops, because it shows that the farmer is listening to the cycles of the earth and educating herself at the same time. Sure, farmers can spray when there's a problem, but every farmer knows that spraying costs money, and it takes a future-thinking person to recognize the best way to grow crops on his or her land.

I get the question all the time if organic wines are better for you. It's not clear to me that they are.

Natural Wines

If a winemaker can produce wine with less environmental impact and make better wine, then it just makes sense. Many wines on the market today are either "organic" or made with "organic" grapes or in some way are "natural" wines. There is an organic labeling on wine, but different rules apply for American labels and international labels, so the term is loosely used in the wine industry. If someone is talking about "organic" wine in our industry, they generally mean no use of artificial/chemical pesticides, fungicides, or herbicides, and no or little added sulfites or other chemicals. Natural wine making is related to this in that, again, there is minimal or no use of any synthetic or manufactured chemicals, but it also says something about the wine making itself; natural wine making means the winemaker uses "wild" yeasts when possible, minimal or no filtering and fining of the wine, and less aggressive use of oak and sulfur dioxide. The goal is to create wines that are "unpolished" that represent the raw, natural terroir of the region.

I purposely lump organic wines and natural wines together, because the philosophies are very similar: to produce wines that are less manipulated by humans and that are ultimately more in harmony with nature in general. There's even an extreme example of this type of wine making called biodynamic, which suggests that only certain parameters are allowed, and it is all based on the cycles of nature, like the phases of the moon. The key is to think of food, wine, animals, and humans in balance and living in the world together and determine how we can avoid hurting Mother Earth. I've had natural wines like the infamous Nicolas Joly's of the Loire with his white Chenin Blancs that are brown rather than yellow after only a few years, and I've really enjoyed them. The reality is I support the efforts, but I don't always drink the product. Many grapes on the East Coast of the United States require regular spraying because of fungus and mildew issues. As a grape farmer once told me, why would a farmer waste money spraying chemicals? They only do so when they have to. In some industries, where agricultural yields are growing consistently every year, good winemakers know that better wine actually comes from reduced yields. The conclusion is simple: you must make a personal decision about natural wine; it both affects the environment and, in the case of natural wine making, the final taste, but that's for you to decide.

Judgment of Paris

In 1976, something amazing happened: American wines beat the French in a blind tasting, and California was rewarded with a permanent place on the international wine map.

It happened in 1976 during America's Bicentennial: America, specifically California, beat France in a wine-tasting competition where French wines were tasted against California wines in a blind tasting competition, and the sole judges were French media and wine people. California won in both the white and red wines categories, so it was no fluke. Comically, often the French judges thought a wine was from France, when it was, in fact, from California, and vice versa. California wines had been illegal in France, or at least it was next to impossible to import them there. The French thinking was, why bring sand to the beach? American wines obviously couldn't be any good, they assumed, so why even bother allowing them into France? Only one news correspondent covered this momentous event, George Taber from *Time* magazine, and although it did get some national coverage in the United States, it was well overshadowed by other Bicentennial activities.

This historic event finally gave the quality of American wine the push it needed. America had proven that the quality of our wines was as good if not better than the benchmark of great wines, French Bordeaux and Burgundy. American winemakers could hold their heads high in international competitions where we've consistently had positive results competing against other international wines. The idea that terroir alone is sufficient to produce a great wine was proven to be false. You also need a talented winemaker with know-how and the ability to get the most from a given location, microclimate, and site characteristics. There is nothing sacred about the great French wine sites. Many wine growing regions in the United States, like Howell Mountain in Napa, California, and the Williamette Valley in Oregon, have fantastic characteristics to make their respective world-class wines. Just because something is French, doesn't necessarily mean it's the best or even good, for that matter.

Understanding the world of wine, even after this decisive blow to French pride, is never easy. You still have to keep an open mind. Just because the French chose American wines over their own, doesn't necessarily mean that the California wines are better. The French claimed that some of the French wines were from lesser vintages that didn't showcase the highest quality of France, but this is, well, sour grapes! Some wine professionals would argue even today that, if the French had the geography and climate of California, they would much prefer the West Coast's wines to the difficult-to-ripen wines of France. What I always pose as a question to new wine drinkers is "what constitutes *better*?" If a wine is judged by itself to be better than another wine, but you're eating a piece of salmon, and the inferior wine tastes better with the food, which is better? My point is, it depends on what your application is. Are you drinking the wine to celebrate all by itself, or are you searing a wonderful piece of salmon with some dill and you want a wine that marries the flavors well?

American Wine

The wine industry has grown quickly in the United States and has created wine tourism and many new jobs in the agricultural sector. The good news is that many regions of the country that were once against booze are becoming pro-wine.

After the *Judgment of Paris* Americans had no reason to fear their ability to create great-quality wine and artisanal products. As the *Judgment* proved, little start-up wineries outside of France could compete on the world wine stage. There is a big growth and expansion of American wineries in all fifty states because Americans are beginning to understand their contribution to the world of wine and food. Maybe a Minnesota or Pennsylvania wine costs a bit more than its French equivalent, but we need to support these wine industries because, ultimately, this will create better-quality products from all sectors. I drink Virginia wines and lend my support to the industry because I know that Virginia wines are an important part of the local economy. Better wine also means better food, and there are better jams, produce, and local products available than ever before. Virginia Viognier (which is a *vinifera* varietal that grows especially well in Virginia) has competed extremely well with French and California versions. Virginia-made Meadow Creek's Grayson cheese is on par with the world's best. American wine can be the world's finest—period!

Bordeaux Copycat

"Meritage" rhymes with "heritage" not "Hermitage." Meritage is California's answer to red Bordeaux.

California has its answer to Bordeaux, and it's called "Meritage." American wine makers use the same five red varietals (Cabernet Sauvignon, Merlot, Cabernet Franc, Petit Verdot and Malbec) to make wines that are comparable in style to the great wines of the Bordeaux region. In California, you can't label a wine by the varietal, say Cabernet Sauvignon, unless it's at least 75 percent of that varietal. Many of California's finest wines are blends of Cabernet Sauvignon and Merlot in the Bordeaux model, with neither constituting over 75 percent, so a label was needed that screamed "Bordeaux-style," and thus was the *Meritage* born. This was a step forward for the California wine industry to identify with one of the world's greatest wine styles. Meritage wines tend to be pricey wines that cost over $30 a bottle and compete for prestige with some of the world's greatest wines.

America Bugs France

Believe it or not, almost 100 percent of French vines are grown on American rootstocks. Back in the 1800s, they didn't have the Internet; in fact, they didn't even have TV, so one of the hot hobbies back then was botany or growing plants for fun. Some American sent a few American vines over to France, a Frenchman grew them on French soil, and the French wine world was never the same.

Everyone seems to have heard parts of this story, but they can't seem to quite understand it right away. A little "bug" called phylloxera came to France via an American vine that was planted on French soil. This is all that Darwinian stuff from high school. In essence, American vines adapted to survive while being eaten up by this tiny little root louse, and they developed enough immunity to continue to produce ripe grapes. French vines like Chardonnay, Merlot, and Cabernet Sauvignon are "vinifera," a different species of grape vine, and they had never built up sufficient defenses to survive through the little bug's attack. Once phylloxera was ashore in France, it began to kill all the vines throughout most of Europe. This was around the time of Pasteur, and the innovations of science and technology that we take for granted today were beginning to sweep the Western world. Still, many French believed it was a curse or some kind of religious guilt trip, and it took many years for them to finally solve the problem: replace all French rootstocks with American rootstocks that have French vines grafted on top. This is how all vines are sold today. You choose your rootstock type, and then you choose your vine type. You don't just choose a varietal like Chardonnay; you can also choose clones that have certain features; maybe they ripen a bit earlier, or need less water, or deal with root stress issues better. The key is, America saved the European wine industry by using scientific techniques to thwart a devastating bug. Does this mean that French wine is the same as American? No, it doesn't; it simply means the roots were formed from plants originally in America.

The fact that the European wine industry was saved is good news for America too because we use the same grafted vines to create American Chardonnay, Cabernet Sauvignon, and other vinifera varietals in the United States. Most native American wine varietals make pretty poor-tasting wine (I've had a decent Norton, but scuppernong, and other American varietals have a "foxy" flavor), and the American wine industry would probably languish if we had to consume solely our native varietals. Science has had many benefits in the protection of vineyards against wine mites, leaf mildew, various molds, and other natural crop devastations and overall has improved the quality and consistency of this agricultural product. On the other hand, technology gone wild has been one of the catalysts for the whole natural movement back to use of fewer pesticides, herbicides, and fungicides; there is significant human dissatisfaction with the overuse of chemicals in the production of wine grapes, as well as other agricultural products and there has been a backlash by many communities against using harmful chemicals to improve yields. The good news is that the residual chemicals in a glass of wine will probably have less effect on you than do chemicals in raw vegetables, because wine making includes heat during fermentation, and most grape growers stop spraying well before final wine harvest.

Thomas Jefferson made a noble attempt to bring wine to the United States and to grow traditional French varietals like Chardonnay and Cabernet Sauvignon. Unfortunately, they all died, and only a little less than a century later would the French find out why.

Phylloxera prevented both the original English settlement of our continent at Jamestown and Thomas Jefferson, the third president of the United States, from successfully growing vines. Nobody had a magnifying glass back then, so they did not know why. The misconception was that Virginia had a similar climate to France and would make an excellent place to produce world-class wines. We now know that the little mite can be prevented only by grafting American rootstocks onto European vines, but we also know that Virginia is not climactically the same as Europe. Yes, today Virginia is making excellent wines, but the reality is that this is partially due to excellent technology and the benefits of modern science. Humidity levels, heat, and rain at inopportune times actually make it very difficult to grow European vinifera varietals here, and only through better understanding of how to deal with these influences have Virginia wines finally attained true class and distinction. Will Virginia ever be Napa or Bordeaux? No, probably not, but I take the opposite position. Can Virginia produce "distinct" wines that express Virginia's terroir?

YOU NEVER KNOW. REMARKABLY, I'VE TASTED WINES MADE IN VIRGINIA AND ELSEWHERE THAT ARE COMPARABLE OR BETTER THAN SOME OF THE WORLD'S GREATEST!

In a blind tasting of three single-varietal wines in a white and a red category, a group of us on a Virginia wine tour were offered a French, a California, and a Virginia Viognier, and the same with a Cabernet Franc-based wine. We voted, not knowing which was which, and the Virginia wine was voted best in both categories.

The secret to understanding Virginia as well as the rest of the United States' terroir is that America has the capability to make the world's greatest wines, cheeses, beers, hams, and pretty much any artisanal food product. All we have to do is spend time and learn about the best attributes of each locale. We have Georgia peaches, Florida oranges, California avocadoes, Washington state cherries, and many other agricultural products that are superior to any in the world, but we still need to spend more time understanding how to produce some of the world's great finished products like prosciutto and Roquefort cheese. Yes, we are catching up quickly, but we are still copying many of the best products. The question is when will Italians or the French taste a Virginia wine or a Vermont cheese and claim it's as good if not better than anything they can make in their own country?

Italy: Never Let the Facts Get in the Way of a Good Story

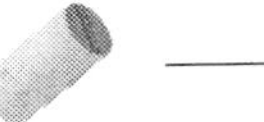

Italian wine classifications go from IGT up to the highest designation—DOCG, Denominazione di Origine Controllata Guarantita. It's not really a designation of better and better quality wines; it really means the wine is more "authentic"...how else can you explain that Asti Spumante is DOCG—the highest quality designation?

In Italy, the rules are different pertaining to just about everything. If you've ever been to Italy, you probably know that Italians love to live life; they are generally a warm-blooded Mediterranean culture. When it comes to naming wines, Italian wines can be named by region, by varietal, or by a little bit of both. It depends on where you are. When it comes to terroir, the Italians are as protective of the status of their wines and foods, as are the French. Many named foods like Parmigianno Regianno,

Taleggio, and Mozzarella di Bufala Campana are protected products, not just by what ingredients are used and how they're made, but also by their geographical limitations of where they can be produced. This is the same with wines such as Barolo, Chianti, and Prosecco, which are limited in where they can be grown and labeled. One misunderstanding that many American wine drinkers hold is that the higher the designation of an Italian wine, the better the quality—this is not true. The designations of quality go from IGT to DOC and then DOCG, the "G" standing for Guarantita. Even though wines with DOCG are the highest designation, this does not mean they're of the highest quality; it simply means the most "authentic." How else would you explain the fact that Asti Spumante is considered DOCG, while many of Italy's highest rated wines—the Super Tuscans—are labeled IGT? Authentic means historically true and expressive of the uniqueness of that region's place—a product that represents the best of that local culture.

Everything is upside down pertaining to wine in the Southern Hemisphere.

Upside Down Wine

The Southern Hemisphere is upside down, so when we have winter, they have summer, and our spring is their fall.

The seasons in the southern hemisphere are the opposite of ours in the north: when it's spring here, it's fall there; when it's winter there, it's summer here. The reason this is important is twofold: 1) Younger vintages make sense to purchase, and 2) winemakers today can get twice the experience by travelling between hemispheres and learning from two harvests a year versus one.

When you look at the vintage label on a wine, Southern Hemisphere grapes are often harvested early in the year, even though the vines were productive the prior year. This creates the strange phenomenon where you can be drinking a very good quality wine in the same year as the vintage. A common example is, since New Zealand Sauvignon Blanc is meant to be drunk young, the grapes that grew in, say, 2008, are being harvested in 2009 and turned into wine and bottled. This means that if you go to the store in 2009 and see "2009" on the vintage label of a wine, that's good—buy it. The wine is fresh, crisp, and ready to drink! Sometimes, just the opposite is true, as well. If I find a wine with a vintage two years before the year I'm purchasing, if it's a white wine I'll often not purchase it. Basically, there's a six-month difference in harvest for Southern Hemisphere wines, so buy them one year younger than you think.

The second point is that winemakers have become international and, just like chefs, they often learn their trade in one part of the world and return to their home to produce wine with newly gained knowledge. The effect of this highly trained wine professional has pros and cons: on the positive side, wine today is better than it ever was before, due to better wine-making skills that include better ways to fight vine disease, reduce bacterial issues, and even better ways to make wine more "naturally" by learning from nature's message; on the negative side, what many older wine writers have said is that wine today is too "clean" and that much of the character of wine has disappeared due to filtration, overripening of grapes (which was more difficult to do in the past), and a more consistent use of oak and other wine-making techniques. There's no right or wrong, but the effect is here to stay. Just as Asian and Latin-American influences have changed the flavors of cuisine throughout the world, winemakers' international experiences mean that the world of wine is more of a melting pot. The differences between the taste of a California Chardonnay and a French one (and for that matter, one from Chile, Australia, Argentina, and even Arizona) is less and less. You don't have to think as much about where the grapes were harvested.

Wines made today are better than ever. You can pretty much go to a store and, starting around $6 a bottle, be assured that you're getting a quality wine.

The question I often get from new wine drinkers is "what makes a good wine?" but the real question is really for you: "Which wines do you prefer?" With literally thousands of great wines available on the market and many of them affordable for everyday consumption, how do you determine which ones you like or dislike? There is no easy answer, but the good news is that you are less likely to find a wine that has a fault or is just poorly made anymore. The trick is to determine what you like, and that can be a problem in itself. I think the key is to make choices based on your lifestyle and, for me, food comes first, wine comes second, and that makes the decision all the easier for me!

Probably the most common wine you'll find me drinking on any school night is Chianti, especially a Chianti Classico. For around $20 or so, you get a red wine with lots of flavor, and it goes great with most foods.

When I think Italian wine, I think Italian food, which just makes sense when you consider their trinity: wine, bread, and olive oil. Another reason is that Sangiovese is the main varietal in Chianti. Chianti is the region in Tuscany, and there's an even better-quality region within called "Chianti Classico." You can up the quality and price one stage when they add the term "Riserva," but frankly, I rarely find the added cost is worth the minimal pleasure difference. This wine was made for food: not too tannic, with nice, earthy, almost charcoal, components, which go great with pork or bacon and great with grilled foods. It has a lovely acidity that gives the wine backbone. I almost always pour this as the first or second wine in the red wine flight at the *Wine Basics 101* class, because it is easy to find in most stores and it goes great with most foods. This is the red wine I drink with the widest range of foods, even if it's a light food like shrimp; add a little paprika and olive oil, and they will taste just fine together. By the way, 2004 was a great vintage, but don't stress about not finding it. There have been mostly good vintages since.

My next most likely wine to drink on an everyday basis is either a Grenache-based wine from the south of France or Spain, or Spanish Tempranillo. Both of these varietals are light to medium tannin and can be drunk young, say within five years of the vintage. Spanish wine tends to label with the varietal, but in France, the southern Rhone region, as well as the Languedoc and Provence, often have Grenache in the blend—suggestion, just ask the person you purchase it from. Wines like this cross the seafood to meat boundaries especially if they are 13.5 percent alcohol or less, which gives them a lighter body and nice acidity balance with food. Spanish food, like Italian, has the olive oil connection, the fat that is not only good for you, but softens red wine tannins—also lots of garlic, which I just love with these wines! Salami, egg dishes, even the unusual salt cod dishes made with *bacalhao* go excellently with simple European rustic reds that are meant for the table, not for storing in the cellar.

Wine Moments...

If you traveled to a quaint little town in Spain and a peasant offered you a taste from his personal wine stash, wouldn't you be curious to try it? Those kinds of experiences can't be duplicated. That is really what terroir is all about, the uniqueness of a personal experience.

Many people I talk to about wine have a special moment when they fell in love with wine, and most often, it's connected with travel to a foreign country. People tend to let down their guard a bit when they leave DC; it's a pretty hard-working town, and eating great food, drinking new wines, and experiencing a new culture, particularly in a European country, opens up the wine bug. The key is to relax and try to explore the local way with food and wine. The only negative that can be gained from this experience is, unfortunately, very common: many people come back to the states and wish they could copy the same moment that happened in that special little place by spending weeks if not months trying to find some special little unknown wine that such and such in the village of who knows where only produces. These people sometimes become obsessed, trying to find that particular wine, when there is no shortage of great wines in the United States. Enjoy the moment; that's what they are, and when you come back to the United States, fall in love again with our great country!

EXERCISE 7: Seat yourself comfortably. Close your eyes and think back to a favorite moment of a trip you took far away from where you currently live. Think about a very pleasant experience you were having while dining and possibly the wine you were drinking at the time. Think about the newness of the experience, possibly people spoke a foreign language you didn't understand. Try to imagine the surroundings in your physical environment such as the plants, people, music, and aromatic smells. Think about how delicious the food and wine were and how you experienced something new for the first time. Accentuate in your mind the features you liked the most and make them larger than life. If there were any people involved, maybe you remember something entertaining about them, accentuate this trait and remember it. This is your "Positive Foreign Wine and Food Experience."

---

7. A MEAL WITHOUT WINE IS BREAKFAST!

No one has ever died from a bad food and wine pairing.

Charlie is ordering wine at a very upscale restaurant in Georgetown. The food is French but very eclectic, because the chef of the restaurant is also a pastry chef who is known for his whimsical style of food presentation and flavors. After receiving the formidable wine list from the courtly sommelier, who is one of the best in his position in the United States, Charlie ponders his decision:

Charlie: "What kind of wine goes with such a diverse array of food?"

Sommelier: "Actually, most people just order a really great bottle of wine that they like and are familiar with."

A Marriage

Wine and food pairing seems to be a complete enigma to many people. The idea, not only that you have to choose a wine but also choose a wine and food combination, seems to put fear in the hearts of many wine newbies. I've never felt this way, because I began choosing the wine for dinners at a young age. That was my *little adult* responsibility. I only knew the white with fish and red with meat rule, so things were pretty simple for me when I began. Over time, I began to hear people in hushed voices suggesting certain pairings that were proper or miraculous and others that I should avoid. Again, I never took much to heart what these people said, and I think you'll find that, sometimes, *rules* are better broken, so read on and enjoy many tried-and-true secrets to pairing, but also some unique Charlie Adlerisms!

In Italy, they eat Italian food on Monday, Italian food on Tuesday, and pretty much every day of the week. So, where do you suppose the wine they drink mainly comes from? You guessed it, Italy! Pairing is easy in European countries that produce wine. But in America, we might eat Italian food on Monday, Chinese on Tuesday, and American (whatever that is) on Wednesday. Pairing wine and food for us can be a chore!

Back to Europe

This is my central premise for the book: wine is so much a part of European culture that pairing wine and food is pretty stress free. If you live in, say Rioja, Spain, you're likely going to drink inexpensive wines from the same region, which is known primarily for reds made from Tempranillo. Tempranillo is usually a medium-bodied wine, not too tannic and not too alcoholic, that has a nice acidity to go with food. Spanish food often has quite a bit of olive oil, pork/ham like Serrano ham, eggs, and local produce that go great with the local wines. In Italy, they drink Sangiovese (the main blending grape in Chianti from the Tuscany region) and other medium-bodied reds like Aglianico and Primitivo in the south that go great with their Mediterranean cuisine. France has regional cuisine and regional wines that go with it. One classic is the Sauvignon Blanc grown in the Loire, which goes excellently with the local goat cheese. Not too far away grows Chablis, a 100 percent Chardonnay that's known for its minerality, which goes beautifully with the nearby oysters.

In America, it's a different story for a few reasons: we are not historically a wine-drinking culture, and we have limited regional cuisine, although that's changing rapidly. I grew up in Harrisburg with Pennsylvania Dutch (actually German) dishes, like chicken potpie and Lebanon bologna, which certainly don't go particularly well with wine. Although there are many regional dishes like lobster from Maine, Tex-Mex from Texas, and Caribbean-influenced foods from Florida, these foods were traditionally paired with the local beverages. It's easy to pair wine with "traditional" continental cuisine like rack of lamb, sole meunière, and tournedos of beef. This was the kind of cuisine that all fancy restaurants had twenty-five years ago, but what wine goes with BBQ baby back ribs or New England clam chowder?

America is all about choices; we don't like to eat the same thing twice in a week, much less every day. Although we eat a variety of foods during the week, most of us would consider it primitive or weird to eat American traditional dishes like fried chicken, steak, and potatoes seven days of the week. Most of us like Italian-style pizza or pasta at least once a week, maybe vegetarian cuisine to lighten things up a bit; Saturday night might mean fancy French cuisine, and Sunday was always Chinese when I was growing up. Although European tastes are changing rapidly, the French generally eat their own cuisine six or seven days out of the week.

Eat Local

Another distinction is that the eat-fresh and eat-local phenomenon has been a part of European culture since its very beginning. In Europe, farmer's markets and produce stands are everywhere, and people traditionally purchase local products such as fruits, vegetables, meats, and cheeses and bring them home to serve to their family; this is done daily, which is how you get the freshest produce, meats, and seafood. Cooking at home is part of the European tradition, and each country and region often has its own style of eating and culinary techniques; you may find butter likely to be part of your sauce in France, cream in other parts, but olive oil is more prevalent in southern Italy and Spain. Up until recent times, grandmothers traditionally stayed at home in Italy and made pasta every day—rolled out by hand with fresh eggs, olive oil, a touch of salt and semolina flour. The quality and flavor of these ingredients are very important to the cuisine, because most dishes are prepared very simply with only a few basic ingredients. As they say with most great cuisine, the freshness of the ingredients is more important than any other component. Fresh means that the food has more flavor and nutrients. Once you put a tomato on a plane and under refrigeration, it loses flavor very quickly.

On the other hand, although Americans do cook, for many years we didn't have the availability of fresh local ingredients, and supermarkets once only carried a few kinds of lettuce and tomatoes, and a limited selection of fruits. This has changed significantly in the last ten years with supermarkets like Wegman's and Whole Foods popping up in the Mid-Atlantic, and many more farmers markets in our region. Still, I've found after organizing over two hundred cooking classes in our region, that Americans generally are less comfortable with cooking and are more recipe focused. This may seem like an unusual difference from our European counterparts, but I've found this to be true when I ask attendees at my cooking classes if they have any questions. I've often seen attendees at these classes take copious notes and ask intricate questions about temperature and ingredients that frankly don't make that much of a difference in the quality of the dish: a European cook would know; an American has to ask. This is not always true, of course, but I've even noticed when viewing the multitude of cooking shows on Food Network that some of the most mundane techniques are repeated over and over again from show to show, such as squeezing a lemon with the cut side up to prevent seeds from getting into the dish.

THEY NEVER SERVE SPAGHETTI AND MEATBALLS TOGETHER IN ITALY, THAT'S AN AMERICAN INVENTION!

America vs. Europe: a Food (and Wine) Cultural Divide

So, what is American cuisine? Meatloaf—yes, fried chicken—yes; but what about pasta or spaghetti? Is that American or Italian? You'll rarely see meatballs and spaghetti served together in Italy. They just aren't meant to be together!

I think it's important for new wine drinkers to understand the differences between European culture and our own, if they want to understand wine and food pairing. One of the most obvious distinctions is how Americans and Europeans are brought up with and perceive food. One of my favorite cinema scenes is from the classic foodie movie *Big Night* when the woman seated in an "authentic" Italian restaurant orders a side order of spaghetti and meatballs with her risotto—a real no-no to Italians, because they never serve two starches together! When I was a kid growing up in Harrisburg, every fancy Italian restaurant like our Lombardo's (I think every town in the Northeast had a similar restaurant!) always served a side order of spaghetti and meatballs before you received your main course. There is a great divide between American perceptions of European (and, for that matter, all international cuisine. Ask my Indian friends!) cuisine and the authentic cuisine of those countries.

Using Italian cuisine as the most obvious example, there really are two different cuisines: "real" Italian and "American-Italian." When immigrants came over to the United States from Italy, they brought their customs and cuisine with them, but they had to make adjustments for the ingredients that were available here in the United States. Meat in Italy had been difficult to come by in the south of Italy, but was plentiful and relatively cheap in the United States, especially after trains began shipping it across the United States in refrigerated cars in the late nineteenth and early twentieth centuries. So many dishes you eat in the United States that are "Italian" should be relabeled "Italian-American." Quick examples include eggplant parmigiana, American thin-crust pizza, and the aforementioned spaghetti and meatballs.

Where's the Taste?

Another food cultural difference is that Americans eat out at restaurants (including fast food and casual) more often than any other world culture, and they eat take-out and frozen or ready-prepared meals. If you're American, you might be eating Chilean grapes, California lettuce, Scottish Salmon, and French cheese all at the same meal. A French person is much more likely to consume foods that were produced nearby. Since Americans spend so much time with premade foods, there is one consistent fact about these foods—they are designed to fit a wide variety of tastes. For example, I've had dishes listed as "spicy" in American restaurants that barely even titillate my taste buds with heat. I'm not a fan of chain restaurants such as Wendy's or Ruby Tuesdays, but they say quite a bit about American preferences: put lots of calories on the plate, serve quickly (the average customer is expected to be in and out in well under one hour), and always focus on adding value/price to the meal—the infamous "would you like dessert" question that every American restaurant server knows to ask or get fired if they don't. I'm always reading food critic chats, and what I rarely see are complaints about food, but people's complaints about service, atmosphere, noise level, and pet peeves constantly come up. Rarely is taste mentioned as an issue. Why should it be? Everyone is expected to add flavor and adjust their own food; this is why condiments are mandatory at restaurants.

Wine and Food Pairing 101

Region First

Pair the dish with the country it comes from. So pasta in tomato sauce, that's Italian, so, think a nice Sangiovese (what Chianti is made of); maybe move up to a Chianti Classico for around $20. You're eating tapas, so go with a Spanish Tempranillo. You can get one for under fifteen bucks. Oysters are loved on the French coast, so go with a nice Loire Sauvignon Blanc.

So think of what country the dish or dishes you're eating originated from—pasta in a tomato sauce is pretty easy, so you can go with a red or white from Italy. But be adventurous—if a Sangiovese works from Italy, how about a Sangiovese from California or Chile? It's worth a try. Roasted meat and potatoes au gratin go great with French Bordeaux, but Bordeaux is mostly Cabernet Sauvignon and Merlot. What about a Cab from Australia or a Merlot from Chile? The basics of pairing a dish with its native wine is you can push the envelope a bit if you know what varietal is involved. French red Burgundy is 100 percent Pinot Noir, and this goes wonderfully with all kinds of game birds and simply roasted meats. Why not try your roasted chicken with an Oregon Pinot Noir? Or mix it up a bit and try a Pinot Noir from New Zealand? Australian Lamb goes great with Australian Shiraz. How about trying that lamb with a French Syrah from the Rhone? The basic principle of pairing wines from the region with foods from the region is to know what the varietal is, and then try that varietal from other regions as well.

Before planes, trains, and automobiles, eating and drinking local wasn't a choice. Back then, shipping was expensive, so you either drank the local wine from the nearby farmer, or you spent lavishly to have your wine delivered.

Technology has made consuming foods and wine from around the world possible. If you go into a modern supermarket, you'll have no problem finding fruit from South America, cheese from Italy, soy sauce made in Japan, and wines from all over the world. Up until the 1800s, only the wealthy could afford many products we consider commodities today such as chocolate, peanut butter, and wine from other than their native country. Even the manufacture of glass bottles themselves was expensive, up until the industrial revolution. Most bottles were hand blown, had imperfections, and, frankly, were in so many odd shapes that transport without breaking would have been difficult. I'm amazed about the story of the original Champagne, which was under such high pressure and the glass was so deficient that the laborers who worked with the bottles had to wear virtual body armor and cages on their faces in case one of the bottles exploded and shattered glass, which occurred about 75 percent of the time! Most wine was usually shipped in the wooden casks and bottled on the premises for the English market, so that they had to invest quite a bit of money.

Most wine consumed in Europe and all over the world for many thousands of years was simply what the local farmer produced and kept in his basement. Wine is a classic value-added beverage—it's how farmers take a commodity product like grapes and turns them into a more profitable product by creating something people want more and are less likely to do on their own. Even in France and Italy today, many people carry their plastic jugs over to a little local winery and fill up; it was once done this way in California as well. Before modern transportation, most people ate locally grown foods in season, because they had no choice, and they drank local wines, because they were readily available.

Go figure—they drink mostly French wine in France!

Local Drink

They don't stress much about drinking
New Zealand wines in France.

The tradition of drinking and eating local products created the pride in ownership that is part of terroir and what makes localities compete to make the best products. Just as a New Yorker will bitch to no end about how bad the bagels are outside of New York (must be the water), a Frenchman will claim that his region's chèvre (goat cheese) is better than that of even the neighboring villages. That cheese comes from a local goat, which was fed on local grasses and vegetation, and its manure was used to fertilize the vines, or possibly it ate the weeds between the vines. The French drink French wine most of the time, as the Italians and the Spanish drink their own wines, not only because it's cheaper for them and readily available, but because they connect emotionally with their own produced wine and cuisine. Being fussy about wine doesn't make sense, because it's something consumed with everyday meals, normally lunch and dinner.

IMAGINE THE BODY OF HEAVY CREAM VS. SKIM MILK—WHOLE MILK IS SOMEWHERE IN BETWEEN

Feel the Body

Pair the body of the food. It's difficult to picture "body," but let me give you a simple way to picture the difference. Cream is very thick and heavy bodied. You can picture how it swirls heavily in a glass and coats your tongue. Skim milk, on the other hand, is very light bodied and thin. Between the two is whole milk, so that would be medium bodied.

Vegetables and simply prepared foods with olive oil or vinaigrettes tend to be very light-bodied foods. You don't want to pair a big robust red wine with a salad, so you need to find a nice, crisp, light-bodied white wine like a Sauvignon Blanc or a Pinot Grigio that doesn't overwhelm the dish. When it's hot outside, most people begin to hit the grill and cook grilled foods like shrimp, fish, and grilled veggies. Because it's hot outside, your body wants to cool down, and you want food and wines that are lighter and more refreshing. It also helps to chill wines a bit more when you're outside; even red wines are nice after you put the bottle on ice for a few minutes. Alcohol tends to show more in warmer wines.

Medium-bodied foods have a wide range. Chicken, for example, in itself is a pretty neutral flavor, but if you were to roast it with herbs on the outside, it tends to get a smoky flavor, and the spices give it a bit more body. The same with fried foods; they tend to be fried in oil, and oil gives more body to food. Tomato sauce, pork, cheese, dark meats, black beans, eggplants, and root vegetables tend to be more medium bodied than crisp veggies, so you need a wine that stands up. My favorite all-around red wines are Tempranillo from Spain, Malbec from Argentina, and Sangiovese from Italy, because these tend to have medium tannin and are not too high in alcohol, with nice acidity to match with the food. Middle-range wines also are nice, because they do fine pairing with lighter-bodied and heavy-bodied foods; at least they don't clash much. Remember—no matter what the food and wine pairing is, the wine needs enough acidity to match the flavors of the food. Chardonnay is the white wine with medium body, and it goes well with richer dishes, especially with butter.

Heavy-bodied foods include roasted meats, steak, lamb, and even dishes with vegetables that have been slow cooked for a long time and have added fat, which can be butter, lard, or just the flavors from slow cooking. In the cold weather, don't you tend to crave stews, chili, and heartier foods to fend off the cold? This is when you want the really heavy-bodied wines like Cabernet Sauvignon, Shiraz (same as Syrah), Merlot, Zinfandel (red), Nebbiolo, and Cabernet Franc. These wines tend to have more tannin and often more alcohol, which makes me think of sitting around the fire on a cold night with a big robust red wine and a hunk of roasted meat! If you're a vegetarian, hard cheeses, and slow-cooked beans and root vegetables, and other braised foods pair well with these bigger wines.

Cut Through Fat

When you think of body in food, think of "weight." Does the dish seem light on your tongue or rich? Fat makes a dish heavy, as alcohol makes a wine weightier.

You can also pair wines that "cut through" the richness of a dish.

If you're eating a dish with a cream sauce or a particularly rich or fatty preparation, sometimes it's better to pair a wine that cuts through the fat and refreshes your palate while you're eating. For example, if I'm enjoying a rich creamy sauce on top of a piece of chicken, I might drink an unoaked Chardonnay or even a crisp Sauvignon Blanc to keep the food alive in my mouth. This is much the same as squeezing a lemon onto a dish after the preparation has been completely cooked. It wakes up the flavor. This is also why a little sweetness in an off-dry wine revives your palate and tends to lighten rich foods. Although this all may seem confusing, because you're not pairing a body to a similar body, think of sweet and sour and how they go together. And have you ever noticed after you eat an especially filling meal, how a sweet dessert can actually lighten your feeling of fullness? Experiment, but especially learn to cook, because this will help you understand flavors better.

SEEK BALANCE IN WINE AND FOOD COMPONENTS

Seek Balance

If you understand balance in cooking a dish, you basically understand food and wine pairing.

Making a dish taste great is less science than art, but there are some rules. Certain combinations work well, while others can disrupt a dish. The key in cooking, as in wine, is to look for a balance of components, primarily those that are sweet, salty, bitter, and acidic. If a dish tastes flat, you can add a little acidity from a lemon or even a touch of vinegar to wake it up. Wine is the same. If a wine by itself needs some life, the winemaker can acidify it to bring out vibrancy. This can also be done by picking some of the grapes earlier before they're fully ripe or, in some parts of the world, acidity is never a problem (think Old World). If a dish is too spicy/hot, then a teaspoon of sugar can make it seem fruitier and less hot on your palate. The same goes with wine, a little bit of sweetness or residual sugar in a Riesling makes fiery Thai food seem more mellow. Higher alcoholic wines also tend to add weight to your palate, so simpler-tasting foods with less spice seem to work better. As all cooks know, you should taste your food as you cook it, so you can adjust the salt and other seasonings. With wine, you can't really adjust the flavors, but you can change the dish a bit to make it go better with the wine.

Old Wine Joke: "I love to cook with wine. And sometimes I put it in the food too!"

Build a Bridge

A secret many chefs know is to "bridge" the wine and the food. The most common way is to simply cook with some of the wine you're going to serve by the glass.

Bridging wine and food is almost like cheating—it works well, even when you forget all the other food and wine pairing rules. If you're cooking or stewing some beef, if you pour a little of the wine you're drinking into the pot, some of the flavors of the wine will be left over after most of the alcohol has been burned off. The wine is chemically changed, but it is also concentrated, which often means it will taste better when you serve the same wine with the dish. As a general rule, restaurants do not cook with very expensive wine—and, in fact, I know of many top-rated restaurants that literally use commercial jug wines just for that purpose. If you're drinking an expensive wine, it's almost overkill to waste a half cup of the fine wine in the cooking sauce, like an aged Barolo from Piedmont, Italy, but you can use either a cheaper Barolo or another rustic wine from the same region of Italy, like a Barbera, to give the dish a similar rustic/Italian flavor to the wine being served.

Cooking with wine does not remove all the alcohol from the dish. Kids have known this for a long time!

Reverse Bridge

You can also "bridge" flavors by adding a component to the dish to match the wine.

The alternative to cooking with the wine you're serving by the glass is to bridge the wine to the dish by adding a flavoring that mimics a wine component. If you have a sweet wine, then you can add some raisins or other sweetener to the dish to match that flavor. Adding green olives, citrus, or vinegar to a dish to raise the acid level can bridge a highly acidic wine. If you really like red wine but you have a light- to medium-bodied flavor like chicken or fish, you can add Kalamata olives, other black olives, or other earthy rich flavors to the dish like rosemary, tomatoes, or eggplants to deepen flavors and make the dish taste much more interesting with a Sangiovese or Pinot Noir. If you have a very fruity red wine with a dish, say a big alcoholic red Zinfandel from California, you can add a little bit of sweetness to the dish to match the fruitiness of the wine. Zinfandel goes extremely well with barbecue sauce. You could bridge the dish by adding the sauce. If you're serving a rustic red wine such as a Syrah from the Northern Rhone, you could add pepper or other herbs or flavors that replicate that spice, so the wine will go better with the dish. These are just a few combinations that pair food to wine components by using a little creativity.

Sauce, Not Protein

Pair the sauce or cooking treatment, not the protein or starch. The reason that people say foods "taste like chicken" is plain chicken has about the same amount of flavor as cardboard!

Shrimp is a pretty light-bodied protein. I think simply of the sweetness and the seafood flavor. If you prepare this simply sautéed in olive oil with some herbs and garlic, then that's a pretty light sauce treatment. I think of drinking a light-bodied, crisp white like a Sauvignon Blanc. If you take that same shrimp and bake it with tomato sauce and feta cheese, as in Greek shrimp Saganaki, you can then easily pair the sauce with a red wine like a Sangiovese. Don't worry about white meat or dark meat. If you cook the food in butter or a rich sauce, say with cream, then you need a medium- to heavy-bodied wine so that you can taste the dish. When I was in Bordeaux, they often added butter to all their dishes, because most of the wine they drink is medium- to heavy-bodied red Bordeaux.

Think in terms of what the most outstanding flavor in a dish is. Chicken is pretty neutral, but if you roast it, you get that crispy skin, which is hearty, so red wine goes great. Salmon is a fatty fish, which goes great with red wine—fat and red wine love each other. But what if you are talking smoked salmon or poached salmon? What about the herbs and spices you're cooking with? Take them into consideration as major flavor contributors. Rosemary is an aggressive, oily, strong-tasting spice associated with lamb, so red wines with some tannin do nicely. Basil can lend sweetness or mintyness like pesto in a dish—maybe a slightly sweet, off-dry wine like a German Riesling.

Think Season

> When it's hot outside, I like wines that are cool and refreshing, and I think of foods that are grilled on the BBQ. When it's winter cold, I think of wines that are great in front of the fireplace.

When the hot summers come to DC, it's not only hot but very humid as well, so the last thing I want is rich food paired with heavy wines. This is when I begin to eat more grilled veggies with goat cheese and more cold plates of charcuterie and olives. I want a wine that is more refreshing, so I can stay cool and enjoy the fresh bounty of the local farmers market. I'm going to stay away from the heavy Cabernet Sauvignons from New World areas like Australia and California and go for lighter- to medium-bodied reds and possibly even chill them down a bit. I don't want any rich oaky whites during hot weather, which is like adding cream to a dish, so I like crisp Sauvignon Blanc or a nice sparkling wine. It's just the opposite when the weather is cold. I tend to eat richer foods with butter or foods that are roasted, and I enjoy wines that warm me up, like Cabernet Sauvignon, Barolo, and Shiraz from Australia. I like wines that are a little more alcoholic, because I'm relaxing and trying to stay warm and enjoying slow-cooked foods that take longer to digest.

Buffer Tannin

Tannins in red wines actually scratch the surface of your tongue and give you that dry mouth feeling from astringency. It feels almost bitter. The best way to soften tannin is the same for wine and tea or coffee—add milk or fat to coat your tongue to soften the texture.

I touched upon this in the red wine chapter: tannin is astringent; it actually scratches your tongue, which means it needs to be softened in some way. The best buffers are fats like cream, milk, butter, or any animal fat or oil that has the effect of coating your tongue and smoothing out the rough tannins. If you're serving a tannic red wine, you can melt cheese on your dish, add a cream sauce, or plop some butter at the end. The French love to add butter to their cuisine both for flavor and to create a wonderful creamy mouth feel, which beautifully buffers red wines. The simple solution to red wine tannins is to eat any type of animal meat, especially game, which has more dark meat and goes especially well with reds. Chicken sounds like white meat, but the fat just underneath the skin and the roasted skin together soften red wines. This is an excellent red wine pairing. Some fish, as well, like salmon, tuna, and swordfish have significant amounts of fat, and this means red wine. The traditional pairing is salmon and Pinot Noir; the tannins from the red wine make the oily fattiness of the fish seem less so.

Mushrooms, Black Beans, and Ghee

If you're a vegetarian, there are other foods that buffer tannin beautifully.

Red-meat eaters drink red wine. It goes with the persona of a brutish cave dweller who hunts down the animal and brings home the trophy to be eaten with a big, bruising, red wine. If this doesn't represent your style of eating, and you're a vegetarian (not a vegan—that's a whole different story!), then you can really enjoy red wine more if you add earthy foods like black beans, mushrooms, and eggplants, which have similar compounds to tannins. Pair these "earthy" foods with red wines with some tannin and they cancel each other out in your mouth. Roasting both meats and vegetables has the same effect of bringing out richer flavors from the umami, and this melds with the tannins of red wines and makes food taste harmonious on your palate. In Indian, Ethiopian, and various international cuisines, clarified butter (also known as "ghee") is used to preserve food as well as making a choice cooking oil. Clarifying butter separates the foamy white proteins that burn at low temperatures from the fat, which can be cooked with at higher temperatures. This is why red wine actually works well with many exotic dishes if they have fat in them. Go with lower-tannin reds, though, if there's hot pepper. This makes reds burn on your tongue.

New Math

I + I = ½. It sounds like funky new math, but it makes sense—everyone here has probably tried a candy bar and a Coca-Cola or soda together. So do they taste less or more sweet together? Believe it or not, less sweet, try it some time.

I heard this years ago at a wine festival in Stratton, Vermont, from Josh Wesson, who was then one of the top sommeliers in the world and the owner of Best Cellars. Taste two similar components together, and they significantly cancel each other out, and in the process bring out the other components of the wine. The most obvious is if you are eating a sweet dish and you are drinking a sweet beverage; the two together taste less sweet than by themselves. I'm not really sure why this is, but probably because your brain's taste center begins to get dulled after a few seconds. How this affects pairing is obvious: sweet foods served with sweet wines become less sweet. This means that a dessert like crème brûlée served with a Sauternes will have an overall effect of less sweetness on your palate. The same goes for bitter and sour—if you have food with a high acidity, like a vinaigrette made with vinegar, then a highly acidic wine like a crisp unoaked Sauvignon Blanc will not only taste less tart, but you will also get more of the fruit components of the wine. In essence, similar flavors cancel each other out, so if you have a really tannic wine and you would like to soften it on your tongue, serve with a food that is also very tannic in flavor. Add chocolate or bitter greens to the dish. For an experiment, try various wines with dishes that have balsamic vinegar as a main flavoring, which affects wine by reducing sweetness, sourness, and savory.

The trick of 1+1= ½ is to think in terms of what food component is the most overwhelmingly obvious in a dish and to pair a wine with that same component. So match sweet wines with desserts; crisp acidic wines with foods with sour components like vinegar, lemon, or lime juice, or other sharp notes; and match foods with bitterness, say from smoke or roasted herbs, with more tannic wines. Frankly, most foods have a balance in flavors, so you don't have to focus too hard on this type of pairing; just remember that a strong component in a food that is not matched by the wine will make the wine taste flat and lifeless. When you match components, the wine shows another side, usually its fruit, but sometimes also its minerality and earthiness.

Another way to bring food and wine together is to adjust the dish to the wine. If you're serving a slightly sweet wine, add a dried fruit component to the dish in the sauce so that the sweet food and wine combination cancel each other out. If I'm in the mood for an earthy, rustic European wine like my favorite Sangiovese, then I add more pepper and herbs like oregano to the dish to soften the tannic compounds or to make the earthy components seem less so. I love to smoke foods using soaked hickory and pecan woods on my Big Green Egg, a wonderful specialty smoker, and this means I choose reds with a smoky component like the Tempranillos from Spain, which see American oak. Adding butter to a simple dish, even at the end of cooking, will make that red wine taste much better together. If this seems complicated, this is simply part of learning to cook better; it's all about balancing the flavors. No one taught me how to pair non-wine cuisines like Indian, Thai, or Sushi. I had to learn the hard way by experimenting!

Sweet and Salty, Sweet and Sour

Dessert wines and off-dry wines pair beautifully with salty, fatty, and highly acidic foods.

Sweet wines can go with sweet foods like dessert, but I prefer to match sweet wines with salty dishes or dishes with a kick of acidity—sweet and salty, sweet and sour. This works because most people enjoy a balance of flavors in food as well as wine. In this case, wine replaces the missing sweet component and makes the food marry in your mouth and nose—sweet, sour, and salty. This is one of the reasons why Asian cuisines go so well with slightly sweet wines. The traditional balance in spicy cuisines is to offset the spiciness with sweet flavors and sour flavors. Whenever I enjoy pad Thai, I always notice the mix of flavors, including the crunch of peanuts, which adds texture, and the sweetness of the soy and sauce. A little sweetness in the wine cuts through the dish's sweetness and lightens the flavors of the dish. With traditional German rich pork dishes, a nice off-dry German Riesling also lightens the dish, cuts through the fat, and leaves a tart finish from the wine.

Smoke and Oak

When oak is used to flavor or store wine in, it lends a smoky flavor for a reason—all oak barrels are toasted with fire to create caramelization so that the barrel stores the wine better and also gives off more pleasant flavors. If you enjoy smoky wines like California Chardonnays that have seen aggressive new oak in their making, then find foods that have smoke as well to offset some of those flavors. I like these wines with smoked foods like smoked blue fish, BBQ pork, and smoked Gouda. It's a limited pairing, but it works.

Acid Test

Acidity in wine is what makes it taste good and go with food. It keeps your mouth alive!

Acidity in food is one of the components that makes a dish taste better. Just as a squeeze of lemon on a dish wakes up its flavors, so can the acidity in the wine you're drinking get your taste buds excited and ready for a meal. This is one of the prime reasons why the French always start a meal with an aperitif, which is usually a crisp, acidic, white wine or a sparkling wine to bring your mouth alive. Acidity gets you salivating and your hunger going so that the first bite of food seems more exciting. This is another reason that high alcohol drinks before a meal are not a really good idea; they will dull your senses. On the other hand, a Scotch or Cognac at the end of the meal with your coffee is a great delight!

Drink What You Like

If all else fails, you can always order a wine that you know you like and a dish that you've always enjoyed, and simply eat and drink them together. Believe it or not, this works most of the time because, at a minimum, you get some satisfaction from both, whether they go together is a different story. This is simple and makes choosing a wine less stressful, especially when pairing a wine makes very little sense. The classic example is if you're sitting in a restaurant with, say, three other people, and everyone orders something different. How can one wine go with all the dishes? If you order a wine that you really like, each person can decide for himself or herself. If he or she also enjoys the wine, it takes some of the pressure out of the decision. Of course, if you're trying to impress a group of people at dinner, always start with a bottle of sparkling wine; it sets the tone and creates a little levity at the start of the meal, making a better all-around atmosphere—plus the sound of the popping cork says time to celebrate!

Charlie: When I was in California, a winemaker told me the perfect pairing for red Zinfandel was BBQ chicken. I can still remember taking the bottle of wine he gave me to a run-down chicken shack, and enjoying one of the finest moments in my food and wine pairing life.

Cheese and Wine Pairing 101

One of the oldest truisms in the wine profession is buy on crackers or fruit, but sell on cheese.

So, one of the common questions I get at TasteDC is what wines to pair with cheeses. Once, when I went to an especially high-end Bordeaux wine tasting, a fellow wine professional admonished me when I went for the cheese before the tasting. Although that's a bit extreme, the point was made: cheese is rich and coats your palate, making it difficult to differentiate between different wines. This is often why in stores they'll serve cheese at a tasting so that the wines will seem less sweet, acidic, or tannic, and the taster will be more likely to purchase. One recent wine study suggests that even wine professionals can't differentiate better-quality wines than lesser ones when they eat cheese; the effect is that overpowering.

When you pair wines with cheeses, the first rule is not to spend too much money, because the subtlety of expensive wines gets lost on the richness of the cheese. The easiest way to pair is to pair the country of cheese origin with wines from that region like the tart goat cheeses of the Loire with their Sauvignon Blanc, or the rich Parmigiano Reggiano of Italy with a Tuscan Chianti, and Brie and a crisp white Burgundy. Another basic rule is that soft cheeses tend to go with white wine and harder cheeses with red, especially aged cheeses like cheddar. Really salty blue cheeses go great with sweet dessert wines and fortified wines like Port and Madeira. The classic English match is Stilton with walnuts and ruby port; this way, you get salty, nutty, tannic from the food (nuts have tannin) and sweet and tannin from the wine. Sparkling wines like Prosecco from Italy and Champagne go excellently with most cheeses, because the bubbles lighten the richness of the cheese. As always, experiment and try new combinations. If you put out a cheese plate, have a variety of cheeses from soft-ripened like Brie, a goat cheese, sheep milk cheese, a blue, and maybe a cheddar or Comté and let people taste a variety of wines.

The easiest food and wine pairing wine is dry rosé; it goes with almost every food. That's why it's the perfect picnic wine, especially if it's chilled.

I covered rosé a bit in the red wine chapter. The better quality rosés are dry and made from barely macerated red grapes. They pair with food so well because they tend to have some of the benefits of both white and red wines: racy acidity and crisp flavors, like white wine, a touch of darker fruit, like strawberry, and a bit of tannin, like reds. Most rosés are light- to medium-bodied, so they go with a wide range of foods from cheese and charcuterie to most seafood and foods with herbs. The other good news is they tend to be pretty inexpensive, and except for some of the top French examples, they mostly cost under $15 a bottle.

Sweet Tooth

If you drink soda with your meals, it's time to stop. People who have a sweet palate have a very difficult time adjusting to dry wines with a meal.

All "sweet tooth" wine consumers can enjoy are sweet wines. They can barely swallow the zillions of dry wines on the market, thus effectively taking them out of the wine market. Sure, there are many good sweet wines, but either they are very expensive, like ice wines and Sauternes easily at $30 or more for a half-bottle (375ml), or they're mostly crappy versions of over-cropped grapes, like white Zinfandel. There are many great off-dry Rieslings under $20 a bottle and some really great ports that are affordable, but this is missing the point: if you want to get into the wine game, then you're going to have to learn to drink dry...or get out of the game! Call that statement controversial, but I meet so many Americans from the South and African-Americans who have a sweet tooth from all the sugar they are acquainted with through their diet: sweet fruit drinks and iced tea with meals, and lots of added sugar in everything from savory foods to extra-sweet desserts. I won't go into the health effects of all that sugar (diabetes anyone?) but 99 percent of the wines carried in wine outlets have less than 1 percent residual sugar, i.e., they are dry. What is the best solution? Wean yourself off the sugared sodas or sweetened beverages (that includes noncaloric sweeteners; they are, in fact, "sweet") with your meals. If you need to get them into your diet, drink them between meals. Another way for the sweet tooth to get into the wine world is to drink New World wines, especially Chardonnays that have spent some time aging in new oak or big red Zinfandels that are high in alcohol. Why? Because higher alcohol tastes sweet on your palate, and the oakiness, vanilla flavor, and buttery characteristics of New World Chardonnays make a wine seem sweeter and richer, often satisfying the sweet cravings.

Spice Up Your Life

Wine is like a spice; it enhances the flavor of food.

If you enjoy food, then wine will come naturally. It's part of the seasoning of your meal. If you think of wine as a way to improve the flavors of food, it can easily become part of your daily meals. What all pairings should offer is some type of synergy, where the total pleasure is greater than just the wine or food by itself. I've given you some techniques for pairing, but don't be afraid to go out on your own and experiment every day. Taste is very subjective; ultimately, it's all about personal pleasure. If you eat out much in the United States, you'll notice that many younger chefs are experimenting with traditional cuisine and pairings and are coming up with new combinations. Frankly, many older chefs don't even think about wine with their cuisine. It's the new young Turks that are really pushing the envelope. It's also not a bad idea to learn to cook. Take a few cooking classes; this will open your eyes to not only food, but also how ingredients can come together.

Taste, Taste, and Taste

The good news is that Americans are really starting to appreciate good food, locally grown food, and produce that's ripe and in season. Whether you eat organic, farmer's market, or you cook most of your own meals, you're part of the new wine consumer—someone who cares about taste!

I had a fascinating experience when I traveled to the Northwest of the United States and visited cheese makers, wineries, and many foodie destinations, including the Pike Place Market. I experienced American terroir! The most memorable moment was at a fruit stand in the market when I was offered a slice of a fresh peach—it was so juicy, that I literally began to choke on the wonderful fruity juices after my first bite. I simply hadn't expected anything that tasted so vibrant and electrical in my mouth! I've had Rainier cherries from Washington State at many Whole Foods in Washington, DC, but tasting them so fresh and close to the source was eye opening and, frankly, even life changing. I'll say it—you need to taste products as close to the source as possible; as soon as you put them in some type of refrigeration and let them travel, they lose something. The essence of flavor is to get to know the source and get close to the producer.

Take a Bite!

Americans are quickly figuring out wine, but don't forget the wine and food connection. Just like the fact that foods from a region go with wines from a region for a reason, enjoying foods that are fresh, alive, and vibrant is important to your wine and food connection. If you learn only one thing from this chapter, please taste your food. With the first few bites of any dish or sample you place in your mouth, allow your senses to really focus on what's going on. Try to relate to the balance of sweetness, acidity, texture, aroma, and flavor components of everything that goes into your mouth, and that includes beer, whiskey, sake, and any other product you begin to enjoy. There is a world of discovery sitting in front of your face; take a bite!

Exercise 8: Think about a food that you really crave occasionally, something that gets your taste buds excited and your stomach gurgling from hunger. Close your eyes and really look at the food item. Imagine how delicious it will taste when you put the first bite in your mouth, really think about the food, but hold back on the first bite. You want to get yourself salivating now, so think about what makes the food so irresistible. Maybe it's creamy and sweet or crunchy and salty, maybe it has a truly magnificent aroma, think deeply about it. Can you detect spices or seasonings, things like pepper, vanilla, fried oil, saltiness, etc.? Now take a big scoop of the food and slowly place it in your mouth and get all the sensations around your tongue and cheeks. Sense the temperature of the food, the texture, and how it coats your tongue or if it has roughness, if you have to chew it, think about how the different flavors come together after each chew. This is your "Memorable Food Sensation."

EXERCISE 9: As an experiment, you are going to experience 1+1=1/2. Find something sweet like a dried cherry or a piece of chocolate, and bite into it while drinking something sweet with it like juice or another sweetened drink. Notice your perception of sweetness in your mouth, does it increase or decrease? Try the same with two foods high in acidity, say green olives and Italian salad dressing. Bitter/tannic is a bit trickier, but you could try dark chocolate and black tea. Notice the change of sensations on your palate and how similar flavors seem to cancel each other out and bring out other flavors. Make a mental note of your experience. This is your "Food and Wine Pairing Experience."

---

8. PURCHASING WINE, OR HOW MUCH IS THAT MONKEY ON THE BOTTLE?

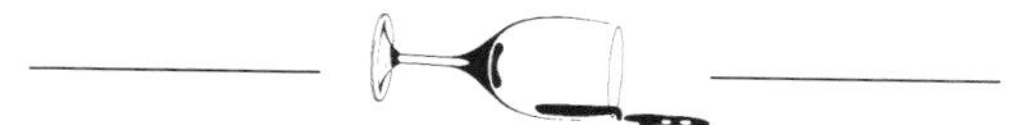

Charlie is in France on a wine trip to Bordeaux in 2006.

Woman on trip: "This is my first time in Bordeaux. I'm really looking forward to this trip!"

Charlie: "Well, it's my second time in Bordeaux, but the first time there were some minor mishaps, like I was pickpocketed and I crashed my rental car, but otherwise it was pretty uneventful."

Woman on trip: "Ohh. That's horrible!

Charlie: "All in a day's job! I'm actually a full-time wine professional."

Woman: "So what's your favorite wine?"

Charlie: "I really like red Bordeaux."

Woman quickly changes the subject.

Costco Situation:

Setup: wide-open shopping aisles at a local Costco with no retail salespeople. A man is looking seriously at a bottle of wine for thirty seconds or so with a quizzical look on his face. Charlie approaches:

Charlie: "I'm a local wine professional, do you have any questions?"

Quizzical Man: "Do you think this would be a good wine? It received over ninety points from Robert Parker."

Charlie: "Well, it's hard to say. It depends on what you're using the wine for. I'm not a big wine critic fan, I never rely on the hundred-point scoring system. I think more in terms—"

Quizzical Man (looking alarmed and suddenly distressed): "How can you say that? It's rated highly by Robert PARKER (voice escalating). You don't know what you're talking about!"

Woman appears from nowhere, consoles man, and speaks to Charlie. "How dare you disagree with this man's decision. You obviously don't know what you're talking about. Robert Parker is a wine EXPERT! He's never wrong!"

Charlie: (sheepishly takes three steps backward, turns, and moves quickly to exit Costco)

Store of Knowledge

If you don't know where you're going, all roads will lead you there. That's kind of what happens when people walk into a wine store.

Over 90 percent of the people who attend *Wine Basics 101* already consume wine at least once a month, so they're somewhat familiar with purchasing wine. Wine is now available in so many retail outlets and restaurants that even Wal-Mart has its own label! Actually, with all the variety available, it's more of a minefield attempting to choose a wine and spend a fair amount of money. There are literally thousands of choices that can be hard to decipher, especially European wines, which often don't tell you much about varietals in the bottle. Add to varietal confusion, different vintages, countries, regions, alcohol levels, oak, organic, biodynamic, and difficult-to-understand labels—what's a Newbie wine consumer to do? This chapter will give you hints on how to better use what you've learned up until now to get what you want. Cut through the confusion and read on.

Wine Shopping

Americans are comfortable shopping for items like shoes, food, and clothes, but they get very uncomfortable shopping for wine. Unlike these other products, you've pretty much committed to buying a bottle of wine once you go into a store; browsing is discouraged.

Once you've walked into a wine store, you've pretty much committed to purchasing a bottle or two of wine. It's so daunting, because most wine or liquor stores carry over two hundred kinds of wine, and they are laid out in many different ways. Normally, there are some shelf-talkers, those little pieces of paper that mention a critic's wine score or certain aromas or flavors of the wine; possibly they tell you what food it goes with. Most stores have specials or discounted wines that have bigger displays at islands or corner locations to catch your eye and stimulate an impulse purchase. In some cases, wine stores allow wine sample tastings, which is a great way to "try on" a wine before you buy, but this is illegal in many jurisdictions and is usually just limited to a few different bottles of wine at any one time, anyway.

According to wine industry data, most people purchase on two criteria: 1) price and 2) an attractive label. Wine marketers take advantage of this—Big Time!

The business of wine is to sell wine—not to educate. Wine marketers look at ROI and other ways to push wine sales, and this is why wine labels use certain colors and graphics to grab your attention, so that you put the wine in your cart and go on your merry way. The popularity of "cute" labels with animals, bicycles, and comedic names to downplay the seriousness of purchasing wine are all directed at the casual wine consumer, who are mostly women. Most of you go through a process of learning about wine by purchasing a wine, deciding if you like it or not, and then purchasing more of the same or similar wines that you like. Frankly, it has to be a simple process, because the same wine is not always available at the store. Since wine purchasing is only a few decades old in the United States, American wine consumers are not as brand loyal as they are to other products: some names like Mondavi, Gallo, and Rothschild are symbolic of quality or value, but the large majority of wine consumers will try something new almost every week. American wine consumers enjoy variety, but with variety comes confusion.

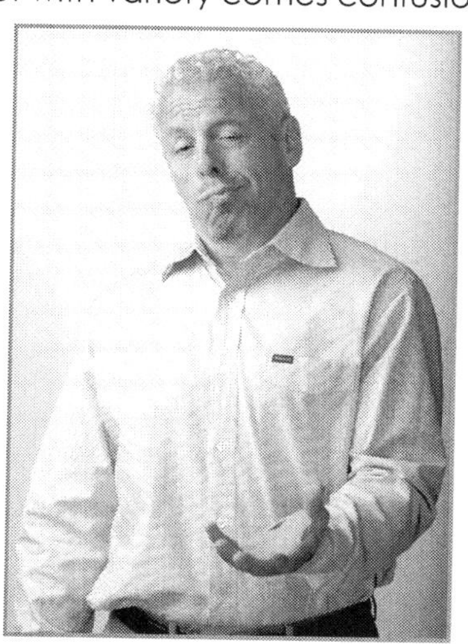

Yeah, right..

B.S.

The wine's back label can say pretty much anything. . .this is the chance for the winery's marketing department to really shoot the bull.

Wine marketing is an advanced industry and everything from the shape of the bottle, to the color and design of the labeling, to the way a wine is positioned in the marketplace is controlled by savvy professionals. This is just a "beware" notice that the back label of a wine is almost totally unregulated by the U.S. government, which gives the winery's marketing department a chance to create that "casual wine lifestyle image" that you're supposed to identify with. Sometimes, it's details about the percentage of varietals used, the types of food that match, or how the wine was made, but often it just builds the wine's brand and image. Comments that wine making "begins in the vineyard," "new French oak," and, lately, a significant amount of reference to "natural" wine making and sustainability are very common. Just remember to take the information with a grain of salt.

Charlie is looking at the wine displays in a concept wine store, where wines are listed by their "style." He overhears a woman asking questions about wine to the store's salesperson and decides to help out:

Charlie: "Miss, hi, I'm a local wine professional. May I help out?"

Woman: "I don't know. I'm looking for a bottle of wine."

Charlie: "Do you have a purpose in mind? I mean is it for dinner or are you entertaining."

Woman: "Maybe. I'm not sure."

Charlie: "Are you just looking for a bottle to have tonight?"

Woman: "I'm not sure. I just want a good bottle of wine!"

Charlie: "Are there any foods you prefer? That might help me?"

Woman: "I don't know. Maybe."

Have a Plan

Don't ask for a "dry white wine" in a store or restaurant. Since 99 percent of all wines sold are dry, this will get you nowhere.

There are around one hundred thousand different wines available at any time in the U.S. market. With so much variety to choose from, you need some kind of plan.

Most new wine consumers walk into a wine store and seem to lose the ability to use their brains. Wine has been so over-hyped because of imagery of sophistication, wine snobbery, chateaux, and images of jet-setting millionaires popping Champagne corks, that the idea of just grabbing a bottle of wine for dinner gets lost in the reasoning. When I talk with wine store representatives, it is very consistent with what questions you ask, and it resonates with the same questions I hear in the class consistently from year to year. Normally, consumers ask for wine with one of the following descriptors: a wine that is...good, dry, not sweet, smooth, sweet, or one that is over ninety points. Obviously, a "good" wine is a matter of opinion. Would you ask an usher in a movie theatre which movie to watch, which one is good? Probably not, you could always ask a friend how the movie was or read a review. Again, it's all about comfort level, because American consumers are so confused about wine, they rely on the help of others more than products they're familiar with. So let's come up with a better approach, a few ideas for a plan that will carry you until you really do know about wine!

Food First

Everyone eats, and wine is meant to go with food, so the easiest preplan to walking into a store is thinking about what you're having for dinner. Food and wine pairing is an important aspect of my job at TasteDC. It's my special niche in the DC area. I'm constantly creating wine dinners and pairings for events. It's almost second nature to me. When you visit a wine store, having an idea of either the dishes you will pair the wine with or the types of foods you regularly eat will help the purchasing decision go more smoothly. If you're a foodie, this is no issue; maybe you already know what ingredients are going into a dish. This will help with finding components in the wine that match, like acidic wines to match the vinegar or citrus in a sauce, or off-dry wines to match the spiciness of a dish. If you're not at that level of cooking or appreciating food, do you at least know the "type" of foods you enjoy? Are you a red meat eater, an occasional meat eater, say mostly chicken and fish, or are you a vegetarian? Do you like spicy hot food or do you prefer bland/mild food? Are you an adventurous eater, always trying new flavor combinations and ethnic cuisines, or do you like just the standards? Do you cook, or is going out to dinner or take-out more your style? Remember, your answer is not right or wrong, it simply tells the salesperson how you choose food, which helps with choosing a wine.

What's the Occasion?

Casual Gathering

One of the best ways to learn about wine and enjoy it is to invite friends over and just open some bottles. If you're pretty new to wine, three wines will normally be enough: a sparkler, a white wine, and a red wine. If you're having a group of friends over and food is potluck or buffet and very informal, serve a red and a white wine after the sparkler. That way, people can choose. Since I'm in the wine business, I always provide all the wine, but of course you can have people bring their own. When choosing wines in a store for a basic party like this, don't overspend; it's ridiculous to serve expensive wines to a wide group of people, unless they are really into wine. This is where a theme for a dinner party really helps—say Spanish tapas, so obviously Spanish wines like an Albarino from Rias Baixas and a Tempranillo would work, or even a hearty spread for a Superbowl where you could choose only American wines. If you have a theme, the wine seller can match according to the types of foods or the mood. This will make your wine shopping experience easier.

Everyday Sparkler

Sparkling wine sets the mood for a celebration. If you don't mind spending $40 a bottle or more, then Champagne works, but there are some excellent sparkling wines under $15 a bottle.

The number one wine I serve as a sparkler at TasteDC events is Prosecco; it's a sparkling wine made from the Prosecco varietal from Veneto, in the northeast of Italy. It's usually a tad sweet, off-dry if you prefer, but it goes so well with hors d'oeuvres and the traditional salty prosciutto and melon (goes great with sushi too), that it's just fun to drink. Cava is the Spanish sparkling wine that is normally dry, but you also get an inexpensive sparkler that goes with so many foods. Salty and fatty foods tend to go with sparkling wines and, since most hors d'oeuvres are both, especially anything with cheese, you should always have some sparkling wines to serve.

Formal Dinner Party

If you're purchasing one wine to pair with a multicourse dinner, some pairing will work and some won't. This is why it's always good to have a red wine and a white wine to serve with a meal.

If you plan to have a seated, multicourse meal, you will need to have more than one wine to pair with various dishes. There really isn't one wine that can match perfectly many different flavors and ingredients. Even if all you plan to do is have hors d'oeuvres, a salad, a main course, and a dessert, at a minimum you should have an aperitif and main wine to go with the main dish. A simple solution that works 90 percent of the time is to start with a sparkling wine, like an Italian Prosecco, Champagne, or Spanish Cava, then move into either a medium-bodied white or a light- to medium-bodied red for the main course. If the main course is light, like a flaky fish or chicken sauced lightly, then a Chardonnay, Viognier, or a Pinot Gris would work for the white. Be aware of the oak in some Chardonnays; if you don't like that style, shy away from richer oaked versions; both Viognier and Pinot Gris rarely see oak. If the dish you're serving is more meat oriented or richer in some way, say the sauce has butter or cream, I love Pinot Noir, Sangiovese, and Tempranillo, but frankly, American tastes tend toward bigger reds like Cabernet Sauvignon and Merlot. Red meat means red wine, so choose lamb or beef if you want to serve a big red wine. If you have to open that Bordeaux red you've been dying to try, get some butter in the sauce, which will bridge it beautifully. For dessert, just keep pouring the main course wine and, at the end, offer coffee and an after-dinner drink like Cognac, Scotch, or Bourbon. I don't like dessert wines with dessert. That's putting sugar on top of sugar. If you must serve a dessert wine, they go surprisingly well as an aperitif at the beginning of the meal, serve it with something a bit rich or fatty, like pâté or hard-boiled eggs in some fashion, and then you get people's palates excited with sweet, fatty, and salty!

Wine Dinners

I've had some pretty amazing wine dinners. I think the most courses I've ever had is twelve, and the most wines with one meal is twenty-eight. I'm all about the food and wine pleasure, but there is something about eating in a historic Chateaux or in a wine barrel room, especially if the speaker is the owner or winemaker.

I don't remember the first wine dinner I attended, but in twelve years in the business, I've attended at least two hundred of them. When I first started out, I was curious about the mysteries of pairing food and wine and how things would taste together. Now I enjoy the camaraderie of other wine lovers, a great speaker, like a winemaker or owner with a story and, of course, really great wine and food. Sometimes, dishes and wine pair perfectly; at other times, not so much. Some chefs are better at pairing than others; never assume that just because a wine and dish were served together that they actually work together. Probably the most memorable was a five-course wine dinner at the Clos de Vougeot in Burgundy, France, the castle of the monastery where all the regional growers had their grapes crushed for many centuries. We saw the original grape press, which was huge, and then we had a wonderful seated dinner with aged Burgundies and Beaujolais too. My favorite dish was simple, which is often true at these dinners. It was morel mushrooms in a creamy buttery sauce with poached eggs; I even forget the wine pairing, the dish was that good! Most wine dinners pair the region's notable cuisine with the region's wine, so if the wines are French, so is the food, and if you're having an Italian dinner, expect the regional wines. Pairing dinners are not only exclusive to wine. I've had dinners with tequila, sake, beer, and even Scotch pairings. I'm an equal opportunity imbiber; I enjoy varied beverages with food! The only issue I have with beer and food is that even though it goes great with so many flavors, beer's much more filling and often I have to slow down—a problem I rarely have with wine.

Food or Wine First?

> A question I often get is should you think about the food before you purchase the wine, or vice versa? It really depends, but if the wine is something special, let the food be in the background.

Most of the time, I focus on food first and treat wine as more like a spice, a food enhancer. Every once in a while, I pull from my wine storage unit a really nice wine and think about the story behind it and when I purchased it. I'm not generally an expensive wine drinker. I mostly drink wines under $20/bottle, but every once in a while, it's fun to treat myself and a guest well with something that has an interesting story. Wine is fun like that. Maybe you meet an interesting person in the wine business and he or she suggests a special bottle, or you save a really high-scoring bottle that is rare or unique in some way. Some people collect wine to show off. I do it to drink better and enjoy it with friends.

The Course, Of Course

The simplest way to pair wine with a multicourse dinner is to have a different wine with each course, and follow the rule: "go from lighter wines to heavier bodied wines."

If you're planning a multicourse dinner with at least four courses, then you may want to follow the European model of serving cuisine: from lightest to heaviest, and finish with dessert. Europeans, particularly the French and Italians, eat many of their meals in courses, which promotes lively conversation, better digestion, and more time to be with friends and loved ones. Courses are much smaller and are normally each served with wine. A basic four-course meal might be hors d'oeuvres, a flavorful salad, a light meat or seafood course, a meat course, and a dessert. Sometimes, a cheese course is added between the main course and the dessert. The key to pairing the wine is to simply follow the weight of the dishes: start with a nice sparkling wine and hors d'oeuvres, then have a crisp white with the first course; proceed to a medium-bodied white or a light bodied red; then move on to a red with more tannic structure and fruit, and then finish with a dessert wine. The French are not really strict about this, even at fancy dinners. Sometimes, a dessert wine is served in an early course, but normally it's red wines after white. Ultimately, food and wine pairing goes back to the

European concept that wine was made to go with food. I've given you ways to match food and wine, and even tips on how to cheat (bridging during the cooking process), so use every tool at your disposal. Remember, no one has ever died from a bad food and wine pairing, and, frankly, most Americans won't know the difference!

What do you like?

In the *Wine Basics 101* class, everyone gets to taste nine wines that differ in many aspects: from sparkling to still, from dry to off-dry, from Old World to New World, from light tannin to heavy tannin, rustic to jammy. Each wine is different and each wine is meant for a different application: some are perfect for food; some are more standalone. If you liked the first wine in the white flight, the Sauvignon Blanc, then stick with Sauvignon Blanc, or drink similar wines that are unoaked. This really helps you when you seek advice on choosing a wine; simply ask for a wine similar to a New Zealand or French Sauvignon Blanc, "and no oak, please!" It sounds simple, because it is. A sales representative generally knows which wine is Sauvignon Blanc and which are "likely" to have been touched by oak. How do they know all this?

Local Experts

People who end up working in a wine store generally aren't paid that well—it's a job of passion. So the sales representative is usually someone who's well read, maybe even a bit academic; they enjoy the interesting world of wine and the people in it.

The cast of characters that I've met selling wine in stores could be a book in itself! Larry, over at Pearson's, Steve at Potomac, Rob at Wine Specialist and, of course, Rick over at Paul's, who's kicked me out of the store at least three times, but always seems so happy to see me come back! When wine became popular back in the '70s and '80s, it was still new and adventurous, and many people got into the business because of the chance to be first at learning about a complicated beverage. As time has moved on, I see lots of twenty-somethings getting into wine and putting their own creative marks on the business. The key is that wine people are about the passion of wine. They're used to answering the same question a million times a day about a sweet wine, or explaining that there *are* sulfites in Italian wines, and answering many other ordinary questions, but most of them love to be engaged with intelligent questions. You might think that you need to carry a wine encyclopedia around just to act like you know your stuff, but that's not true at all; keep it simple, and just try to express in lay terms what you want, like this:

"I'd like an inexpensive sparkling wine under $20 for a romantic occasion."

"I'm a vegetarian. What red wine do you have that goes great with Mediterranean cuisine like grilled or roasted vegetables?"

"I'm looking to celebrate a special occasion with a wine lover. Do you have any nice Bordeaux in a decent vintage for, say, under $40 a bottle?"

"I'm just starting out, but I just came back from Napa and I really like Merlot. Could you set me up with a variety of wines?"

Define Your Style

"So after tasting a French Bordeaux red and a California Cabernet Sauvignon, you probably like one style more than the other. If you like big reds that say *fruit*, big time, then New World is your style. Try wines from places like Chile, Australia, California; if you like wines that are a bit earthier and more rustic style, choose wines from France, Italy, and Spain."

Style is very personal with wine; it relates to your background and how you approach life. If you purchase shoes, you know your style: who the designer is, who else wears them, what they should cost, what dress they match or if you need a dress to match them, where you would wear them (party, office, date, or anniversary), and if now is the time to buy or if it's better to wait for another time. To define your style, always consider the application: is the wine for everyday drinking or a special occasion, do you want red or white, do you have a food match in mind or will you just drink the wine like a cocktail, and what are some wines you've liked in the past? At *Wine Basics 101*, most people find a couple of wines they like and a few they don't care for—this is the importance of frequently going to wine tastings. The more you taste wine, the more you can determine what you like for purchase.

The more familiar you are with your wine style, the easier it will be for the salesperson to lead you in the right direction. Surprisingly, most people walking into a store have the same questions over and over again; they are not particularly helpful in their own purchasing decision. Here's an important note at this point: it is not the job of a wine seller to listen to your stories, hopes, and dreams. In the wine business, we seem to hear these intimacies from consumers more than our fair share. The ultimate goal of a sale is to make the exchange and hopefully create a regular satisfied customer. You may think it's important that we hear about your recent trip to Italy, or whom you know who is important in the wine business, but the wine retailer's job is just like salespeople selling you jewelry in a store—they take your money and say, "Thank you."

The simplest way to direct the purchase is, if you drink a certain producer's wines or a given region, say that you really enjoy Bordeaux. Bordeaux is well represented in almost all retail outlets, because they produce significant quantities of wine, and it's the benchmark for so many great wines. Since the reds are primarily Cabernet Sauvignon and Merlot, you could also ask for a wine with those varietals from another region. Once you know what you like, you can redirect a purchase to fit your needs. Some people like only sweet wines, so they can go directly to the dessert wine section. Some people love loads of fruit, so a real fruit-forward wine like an Australian Shiraz or a California Zinfandel will satisfy that urge. There are literally thousands of producers and hundreds of wine importers, so I don't suggest memorizing too much detail about them. The number one reason is you never know if their wines will be available in the store. There are exceptions, though.

Some importers are specialists in representing small producers or other regional wines. They're always good to go to for wines that show character.

The DC area has some really great wine importers, like Fran Kysela, Robert Kacher, and Aurelio Cabestrero, who each specialize in niche markets. They have a high trust factor because they live locally and are well known by many in the wine industry from sommelier to street rep for consistently choosing wines that are very good for the price. Importers are one thing, but trying to follow producers is a whole different story. I've heard too many stories of unhappy wine consumers who want a specific wine producer's wines and, for whatever reason, they can't get them. Sometimes, they become outraged and obsessed, and frankly, this is why I want you to avoid stressing about who makes the wine. The good news is that there is very little reason for wine retailers to sell bad wine—yes, occasionally, I'll get a wine that isn't as good as expected, but that's the exception, not the rule. Because the wine business is so competitive, you can bet that most wines are pretty good at their price and quality. The biggest value shortfall is when you purchase cult and boutique wines.

Buyer Beware

Just because a wine is expensive doesn't mean it's good or worth that much. It's kind of like one of those expensive Jimmy Choo bags. Does it hold your things better than a much cheaper bag? No, it's simply fashionable. And can you justify a Rolls Royce price tag by the quality of its smooth drive?

Many of you think that an expensive wine means it's good—but how could you justify paying over $1,000 for a single glass of wine? There are about five of those in a bottle. The reason Domaine de la Romanée-Conti costs that much is that some people can afford to have four homes, a private jet, and pretty much whatever else money can buy.

The number one reason that wine can be very expensive is economics, not quality. If people want to pay $400 for a bottle of wine or, for that matter, $4,000 for the same bottle of wine, that's because they feel it's worth that much. Certain wines like cult wines from California, top-growth Bordeaux and rare Burgundies, often command these kinds of prices and, often, you can find older vintages at auction. The more rare or more prestigious the label, the more people will pay. Vintage makes a big difference as well because certain years are rated higher by the critics and will sometimes double or triple the normal price.

Don't be ashamed if you never can afford to drink a bottle of wine that costs more than say $200 a bottle or so; you're not missing much, I know. I hope you realize that wine is a simple pleasure to enjoy with a meal; crack the screw top and pour with your meal!

Make a Relationship

The best way to learn about wine quickly and get the most help is to make a friend with your local wine retailer. Not only will you get assistance from a live human being, but you will also get the scoop on the wine, and possibly a better price deal. Most stores now have e-mail newsletters and it's a good idea to subscribe if you like to learn about wine at your own pace and possibly save some money. The value of the relationship is that you can open up and ask questions that you may be embarrassed to ask a stranger; you'd be surprised at how much confusion can disappear just by asking.

Wine Specialists

In Washington, DC, Virginia, and Maryland, there are many different stores that specialize in different types of wine. One store might be for high-end rare wines, another is known to have a broad selection at discount prices, and others are known for unique wines from newer wine-making countries. I think the people who sell you the wine are more important than the store itself, so it's always worth trying a new store every once in a while. I tell new wine drinkers to mostly stay away from purchasing wine at the big Costcos and supermarkets when they start out, so that they can learn firsthand from people who will get to know their names and talk to them. I need to mention a bit of store etiquette. If a salesperson spends time with you, not only should you buy wine, but you should also buy a few bottles. This gesture says to the employee that you're serious about learning and that you will take his or her advice and experience different wines. Remember, you should always have a few bottles available at home for any food emergency!

Get Some Value

The best value in wines right now is from South America, specifically Argentina and Chile. With cheap land, labor, and a pretty strong dollar, you can get a decent bottle of wine for around $10 or so that matches wines priced twice as much elsewhere.

Why pay a lot for wine when there are some really great deals? Actually, every country and region generally has good values in wine; you just need to learn to be a smart shopper. Yes, some Bordeaux cost your weekly paycheck, but there are so many Cru Bourgeois and Cru Superiore made from mostly Cabernet Sauvignon or Merlot, and they go great with food. Burgundy is notoriously an expensive wine, but French wines from less-well-known regions like Alsace, Languedoc, and the Loire can be good values. I consider a "value wine" a wine you can afford to drink every day, which for me is around $15 a bottle or less. You can even do better than this by purchasing at discounters, but I really push new wine shoppers away from faceless big stores; it's still better to make a relationship with a human being at a wine shop. Right now, I'd say the best values in wine come from South America. There are some really great Chilean Cabernet Sauvignon, Merlot, Sauvignon Blanc, and Chardonnay, often for around $10 a bottle, maybe a bit more for the reds. Argentina, too, for Malbec, which is a French varietal they produce. They do a great job with Chardonnay too.

The price of wine is totally affected by supply and demand, and right now, with the world economy in a freefall, there are good deals available from all over the world. This is another reason you should consider purchasing a few bottles at a time and storing them away in a dark cool place. Some retailers offer discounts on purchasing cases, sometimes mixed, which gives you a chance to try an assortment of twelve different wines. Just as with any other item, it's fine to price shop and, yes, ask the retailer how you can get a discount; many will do so, especially in DC!

Internet Wine Purchasing

I subscribe to most of the major wine retailers' newsletters and a few daily-deal wine sites, because I always like to see what's available in the market and at what price. A smart wine consumer is also a good price shopper; you never know what deals might appear. If I have a specific wine in mind, I go to www.winezap.com or www.vinfolio.com. I have the premium service at www.wine-searcher.com. Remember, if you purchase wine over the Internet, they have to ship it and that usually adds about $3 per bottle to the cost. For inexpensive wines, it often just makes more sense to go to your local store. On the other hand, retailers need to clear their inventory all the time, and great deals can be found. The good news with wine is that every year there is a new vintage, which means the old one has to get off the shelf. Some vintages are popular because of great scores, but lesser vintages are often great values and actually go better with food.

It's a Gift

I have mixed feelings about purchasing wine as a gift: unless you really know the person you're purchasing it for and the types of wine they like, buying wine for someone you don't know has some risk. On the other hand, I think almost everyone likes a bottle of Champagne, so that's something to celebrate with at any time. Gift wines tend to be expensive, because you're suggesting that you're purchasing for a special occasion like a birthday or the holidays.

Use Ratings, Reviews, and Shelf-Talkers

Robert Parker is the nine-hundred-pound gorilla of wine critics. He is so powerful that he can actually make or break some of the world's great winemakers depending on how he scores a wine.

Using wine critics' scores to choose a wine is a safe bet if you trust the wine reviewer's palate. Two wine reviewers are by far the most influential in the U.S. market, Robert Parker and his *Wine Advocate* and the wine staff who work for *Wine Spectator*. Both of them use a hundred-point scale where any wine rated ninety or higher is considered to be very good; it's sort of like getting grades in school. Parker actually got started pushing his wine newsletter at a DC wine store and grew from there. His big claim to fame was when he scored Bordeaux wine futures high in 1982, when other critics were less than excited by the vintage.. Over a few years, he proved he was right and became a worldwide wine critic legend. *Wine Advocate* gives complete descriptions and reviews of many top-rated wines but most people ignore the text and go right for the scores. You can even subscribe to www.erobertparker.com and sort wines by score alone among other criteria. *Wine Spectator* is actually owned by Marvin Shanken, a former Wall Street investment banker, who turned the *Wine Spectator* into the world's most circulated lifestyle magazine with over two million subscribers. Reviewers at *Wine Spectator* like James Laube, James Suckling, and Harvey Steiman have become very influential over the years and their scores have a wide influence on the price and prestige of many wines. There are other wine reviewers in the marketplace, but these two publications have the most significant influence on American consumers' perceptions of wine quality and value, and ultimately how wineries market their brand and products.

Many stores list scores on their shelf-talkers from either of these publications, as long as they are close to ninety points or above. It's an effective marketing tool; many people simply purchase based on this alone. It's an easy way to choose a wine if you like wines that show well in tastings, which generally means they have more powerful flavors, often from higher alcohol and intense fruitiness. I mention in the prior chapter the "international wines," and these are actually made in a way to get higher scores by pulling riper fruit, long use of barrel aging in new French oak barrels, and many other chemistry tricks that can make tannin seem much softer on your palate. Just remember, a high score doesn't mean you will like the wine, and it doesn't mean it will go better with food. I use the scores simply as a way to suggest that this wine impressed a critic in some way. Sometimes, the two publications disagree and often a ninety-plus point wine in one publication scores much lower in another.

I often use the store representative like a wine critic, but you have to know how to ask the questions. Since wine stores don't normally score wines, what I try to determine is how it relates to other wines in the same style and price category. If I want to spend only $15 for a bottle of wine, say from Rioja, Spain, I want to know from the salesperson which Rioja around $15 is her favorite and will go best with the foods I would eat it with—tapas in this case. In this way, I direct the answer to my question rather than simply relying on a purely subjective score.

Get Educated

I've been organizing wine classes and food events with TasteDC in our region since 1997, and I'm amazed at how people here have progressed in their wine knowledge. When I first started out, wine was still a mystery to most people in our region. Now it seems that, with all the wine classes, tastings, and information available, many people have figured out wine. As with any complex product, I suggest that taking classes or going to tastings is a great way to learn, as well as a good way to update your knowledge. Most tastings are oriented either toward a wine region or a type of wine, like Pinot Noir or rosés, so that you can compare and taste. Some tastings also offer you the chance to purchase or order wines for future pickup, which kills two birds with one stone.

Wine Tastings

Since I make a living teaching and organizing wine tastings, I know the value of a good class. You can choose seated wine classes with instructors, but many events are also walk around/reception-style tastings, where there is no speaker; you just taste at your own pace. Either way, a wine tasting gives you a chance to sample before you buy and also to ask questions about the wine. When I began over a decade ago, there were only a few tastings a week, but now, with so much consumer interest, there are probably two or three tastings a day in our area, and some of them are free. Some tastings include food or dinner, while others don't. You should take that into account in the price of the event. When I organize a wine class, there are normally seven to nine wines to taste, and you are seated. Those events take approximately two hours. Standing reception events often have twenty or more wines, so you may want to spit, but definitely have something to eat at the beginning. Each tasting is very different based on the organization and the speaker involved. I like to think that TasteDC events lean more to the fun and casual atmosphere, and we tend to focus on the food and wine connection. Many wine groups keep e-mail newsletters like stores do, but you can also use www.localwineevents.com; they have a good diversity of wine events.

What's Your Age?

Indirect quote from Robert Whale, Australian wine importer: "There are three kinds of wine drinkers: French, English, and American. The French, well, they like their wine young, very young; in fact they like everything rather young. The English are just the opposite. They like their wines aged for a long time, sometimes way past their prime. And Americans. . .well, you have no idea how long to hold a wine; you have to ask someone! This is where Robert Parker fits in."

I always get the question: "How long should I age a wine?" My answer is, "It doesn't really matter, anyway, because 99 percent of all wines are consumed within forty-eight hours!"

The process of aging wine is still a mystery. Since most wines have cork stoppers, the question is, how can a wine age in a bottle? The assumption is that the little bit of air at the top (in the "ullage") helps the wine change. The "how" and "why" are still question marks, but there is no question that a wine does, in fact, age in the bottle, and some of its characteristics change: both white and red wines begin to lose some of their up-front fruit flavors, and white wines get browner, while red wines become brick colored.

A critic says, "This wine will age for six to nine years," but how does the critic know? It's just an estimate; maybe the critic has had a similar wine, but only time will tell. I like the solution that the English invented: buy a case of twelve bottles of the same wine and open a bottle every year until it's ready!"

Ninety-nine percent of wines made today are not meant to be aged, and, actually, some wine like Sauvignon Blanc is better very young. Most reds age up to five years and whites up to three years.

Wine is meant to be drunk young and with food—that is the primary purpose of wine. The fact that some wines are "age-worthy" simply means that they have more "stuffing" than other wines. For example, in Bordeaux, they sort grapes carefully after harvest to get the most ripe and unbruised grapes to put into their better wines. These grapes are then fermented, and sometimes even soaked in order to extract as much of the concentrated skin pigments and tannins as possible. These are, in fact, what helps the wine age. Other factors that help preserve a wine longer include higher acidity and the sugar in wines. Port, Madeira and other fortified wines age extremely well because they have plenty of sugar and added alcohol, which allow them to age for many years. Dessert wines like Sauternes and late-harvest wines also age extremely well because of their high sugar levels. They go from being yellowish in color to brown over many years and gain a nuttier flavor, sometimes like toasted hazelnuts. Why age a wine? Because tannins tend to soften or drop to the bottom of the bottle (it's called sediment because you can actually see it's almost like mud!) and the wine becomes more interesting and integrated. A simple analogy for red wines is young vs. older wines are like red wine vinegar to aged balsamic vinegar. In fact, the processes of using oak and aging are similar in both. Aging mellows the tannin in wine, brings out secondary characteristics like earth and herbs, and increases umami/savory. Food wise, an older wine has much more subtle fruit, so I like older wines with foods that aren't overpowering in flavor and those that are roasted with herbs as well.

And what happens to you if you drink a wine too young? Actually, nothing, you'll be fine! A younger wine simply doesn't show the full range of flavors, but if it's a well-made wine, it will show lots of intense fruit and a long length on the finish. Although the wine critics love to put in their reviews the "optimum" window for aging, this is only an estimate, which is usually based on past experience with the wine. Some wines really do age for a long time: top Bordeaux, Barolo, and Barbaresco from Piedmont, Italy, well-made Burgundies (both white and red); dessert wines and fortified wines age especially well because of sugar and/or lots of alcohol.

Needs to Breathe

There's an old French proverb that says wines are like people: when they are young, they need to run around and breathe, but when they are old, you better listen quickly!

This is one of the top questions I get and one of the most confusing to understand. A wine "breathing" means that it is opened and allowed sufficient contact with the air. Wine "breathes" because its aromatic compounds and alcohol open up in the air and release some of their intensity. No—I can't scientifically explain it, but from experience, I can say it really works. If you have a young wine, especially a red, pour it out of the bottle into an open container; a decanter or pitcher works fine, but a big glass is good as well, and give it a few hours. The wine will soften, and the tannins and alcohol often seem less aggressive and make the fruit and other wine concentrates show better. Do you need an expensive decanter? No, it's about the open air; it doesn't matter what kind of container. You just need air exposure. Can a wine breathe if you pull the cork out and let it sit? No, not much anyway, the surface area of an open bottle of wine is minimal, and certainly not enough to get sufficient air contact with the wine for quick breathing. Why shouldn't you let an older wine breathe?

You decant a wine for two different reasons: 1) if it's a young red and needs time to breathe or 2) it's an old wine and you want to get the sediment out.

OK, so this is not very important, but it's a distinction that I make all the time, because I get the question all the time. Older wines are more delicate; much of their flavor concentrates and tannins have dropped to the bottom of the bottle and formed sediment. If you let an old wine breathe, it runs out of gas, literally and figuratively, so that all the wonderful flavors are gone. On the other hand, if you don't like muddy sediment in your mouth, it doesn't hurt to decant an old wine and then pour it carefully into the glass. There's actually a simpler solution: just stand an old bottle vertically and leave it that way for a day or so, and all the sediment will drop to the bottom. Just pour it out carefully into the glass. What happens if you drink a little sediment? Nothing. I actually think it makes the glass of wine more interesting!

Aging and breathing are not the same,
but air is involved in both.

The question comes back, "What wines need to breathe and what wines age?" It seems like I've already touched upon the answer, but there's a reason I don't like to give too many details—it's just one of those personal things. For example, some people like wet-aged steaks, some like dry-aged, and some like them dry-aged for a long time, say twenty-one days or longer. Just as with wine, the process of aging a steak completely change the flavor and aromas. Which is better or which is the proper aging period? That's a personal decision. I can't help you. My job at TasteDC isn't to tell you what's right or wrong, it's simply to help you make your own decision. In the end, it's all about *your* sense of taste.

DON'T SNIFF THE CORK!

Restaurant Wine

When you go to a fancy restaurant and you ask for the wine list, you get what seems like a twenty-pound encyclopedia handed to you by a guy with a silver medallion around his neck—of course you're intimidated!

Don't sniff the cork—it smells like cork and you might get mold on your nose. People will laugh at you.

I don't think there's anything more stressful in life than ordering wine in a fancy upscale restaurant! Most people go out to fine dining rarely because of the cost, and it is often some type of special occasion like a birthday, anniversary, or possibly just for business, but the wine purchase can be very tricky. First, there tends to be a wine list with hundreds of wines. How could you possibly know where to start? Some wine lists break down by the type of wine, like "light-bodied whites," which definitely helps if you know what you're going to eat, but often the wine list is offered and the order taken before you've ordered your food. The first trick of ordering wine in a restaurant is to relax—you're not expected to know all the wines; that's why they hired the sommelier. Let her help you!

Somm...What?

Definition: sommelier (from Wikipedia), or wine steward, is a trained and knowledgeable wine professional, commonly working in fine restaurants, who specializes in all aspects of wine service. The role is more specialized and informed than that of a wine waiter.

Traditionally, sommeliers were more like wine managers, and their job was to make sure the cellar had a range of quality wines stored properly. Only in recent years did wine and food pairing become part of the job.

A sommelier's job is prestigious, especially in the United States, because it represents what people expect from a fine dining experience: a touch of class. The role goes back to the days of butlers and English and French castles, when the wealthy showcased their status by having servants and other signs of wealth. When restaurant dining became more popular in the late nineteenth century and on into the twentieth century, fine dining establishments knew that having a sommelier would create prestige for the restaurant and attract a better-paying clientele. Since cuisine in the old traditional restaurants was based on European cuisine of the time, many rich cream sauces and relatively heavy preparations by today's standards were offered, and the rule "white with fish and red with meat" applied. Today, not only has cuisine changed, but so has the role of the sommelier. They not only manage the wine cellar for a restaurant, but they often get asked to pair wine and food combinations. My experience is that some do a better job than others, but it's a trickier job than it may seem. How do you pair dishes from various diners when they have a wide range of flavors? The easiest solution is to either offer a red and a white wine with the meal to satisfy everyone or to offer wine by the glass, so that each person can choose. Most sommeliers would probably agree that the best thing to do is to choose a wine everyone at the table is happy with, and often that means a big red. By the way, you are supposed to tip the sommelier as part of the meal. I just add it on as a gratuity on top of the wine.

Wine Markup

Restaurant markups are notoriously 200 percent to 400 percent over their cost. It's closer to 50 percent over cost markup in retail outlets. Therefore, choose carefully in a restaurant.

Then you look down the list and notice the prices of the wine; some wines are well over $100 a bottle, some even cost thousands of dollars! The next question in your mind is probably how much you should spend. What is a good wine for the occasion that won't break the bank? The basic rule of restaurant markups is that lower-priced wines tend to be marked up at a higher percentage. For example, if you order a $40 bottle of wine in the restaurant, this usually has the highest percentage markup. I've seen wines that sold wholesale to the restaurant for $8 marked up this high, but, normally, a bottle of wine you can purchase retail in a store is approximately double that cost in a restaurant in the United States. Higher-priced wines have lower markups percentage wise, simply because most people won't pay a huge premium just to dine out.

When you go to a restaurant and order a wine off the wine list, check the vintage closely. Different years can make a big difference in price due to restaurant markups. And definitely check the label when the wine is delivered; often the wrong vintage gets delivered.

In Bordeaux, 2005 was a great vintage; the wine gods gave the region great weather and even better wines that were scored very high by Robert Parker, the wine critic and powerful guru of high-end wines. In 2004, the year before, an older vintage was not nearly as good; in fact, it's called a "classic" vintage because Bordeaux got its more normal rainy, cool, and difficult weather making the grapes not quite as fully ripe at harvest time. Prices for these two vintages are so different that you could pay three or four times as much for the same producers' wine from 2005 than you would for their wine from 2004. For example, one of the top-scoring wines of 2005 was Ausone, which, in early 2009, is selling for over $2,000 a bottle at retail stores, while the 2004, which was scored significantly lower, sells for only around $500 a bottle. This is just to show an example of price disparity between different vintages. Personally, I think these prices are pretty outrageous. You really don't need to spend anywhere near that much, but be wary of how you can be easily fooled in a tense situation.

Corkage

Some jurisdictions in the United States allow you to bring your own wine, and they charge what's called a corkage fee. In our region, it's illegal in Virginia and Maryland, but allowed in DC.

Most people rarely bring their own wine to a restaurant, and since so many restaurants carry such great wines now, there will probably be less and less need to do so. Normally, the corkage fee is somewhere between $10 and $50 a bottle, plus you pay tax on top of that, and you should tip as well. The basic rule of bringing your own wine to a restaurant (more etiquette than rule!) is that you should not bring a wine that is available on a restaurant's wine list, and you should offer a taste to the manager or sommelier once it's opened. Some people say you should also purchase one bottle of wine from the restaurant if you bring your own. I think that's up to you. The basic point is to bring only a wine that is collectible or special in some way. It's ridiculous to bring an everyday wine just to save money, because the purpose of a corkage fee is to allow you to taste the restaurant's dishes with a special wine not readily available. It's a classy move to do this occasionally, but again, restaurants are in the business to make money, so you shouldn't use this simply as a cost-cutting measure.

Restaurant Ordering 101

Ordering wine in a fancy restaurant is scary, especially if it's a special occasion. I suggest starting the meal with Champagne—the sound of the popping cork puts everyone in a mood to celebrate, and the bubbles are so refreshing!

The Wine List

Wine lists can be pretty extensive at a fancy restaurant, and this makes sense because often 20 percent or more revenue comes from beverage service. Wine lists are organized many different ways: some by country; some by type of wine like white, sparkling, red; and others include descriptors. All list price and, often, it's in descending order—a trick used by the sommelier so that she can gauge how much you "really" want to spend, which makes sense when dealing with a new wine-drinking public. At a fancy restaurant, you can expect literally hundreds of wines, so there is really no expectation that you know or have ever heard of most of the wines. You just want to form an "idea" of what you want. Some restaurants have their wine lists on their Web sites, so this is an opportunity to preselect wines, but I think that's overkill. The most important thing to do in a tense wine-buying situation is—relax. The best way to build confidence in your decision is to realize that there is no way you could know about all these wines. Even a wine professional like me hasn't tasted more than 20 percent of the wines on most lists. The sommelier is there to help, and often he or she hopes you have a love of wine. It's the sommelier's job to know the wines on the list, not yours, and a good sommelier will assist you with your decision.

The wine list is normally given to you early in the meal; sometimes it's even with the menus when you are first seated. Since, at that point, you don't know what dishes you'll be ordering, I suggest you wait to order the wine after you've chosen your dishes. Ordering the wine afterward makes more sense. Food and wine matching is the most sensible way to order a wine at a restaurant; you're there to enjoy a nice meal; the wine should be part of the experience. The exception is sparkling wine or

Champagne, which you can order at the very beginning; in fact, that's an excellent way for everyone at the table to loosen up a bit and celebrate!

Tiny Pour

The sommelier will pour only a little wine into your glass so that you can decide if the bottle is "good" or "bad." The sommelier is not really expecting you to see if you "like" the wine, only if the wine has a fault and should be sent back.

After you choose a wine and the wine is brought to the table and the cork is presented to you, the sommelier will pour just a little bit of wine at the bottom of your glass. This is the point when your tasting lessons from chapter 2 become useful. You're simply expected to sniff the wine to see if it is corked or has another fault, and to give your approval so that the wine can be poured for the rest of the table. The reason the pour is so small is that you can actually tell more from a little splash of wine because it gives the glass more room to aerate its aromas—the classic wine glass as aroma chamber. The best way to get the most from this experience is to give the glass a good slow swirl at the table a few times before you put your nose in for a good sniff. This is your chance to focus on the aromas of the wine and to do a quick evaluation: is this the wine you thought you ordered and does it remind you of any wine you've ever enjoyed in the past? The process of swirling, nosing, and tasting a wine is a chance to get in touch with your past sensory experiences and memories. If you're new to wine, a good sniff or two and a sip of wine to taste will tell you all you need to know: whether the wine has a fault or not. As you gain experience and confidence in your tasting abilities, you will be more relaxed in restaurant situations. I find the moment of tasting to be a quick break from the outside world, a chance to transcend the ordinary and enjoy life's pleasures!

If the wine has a fault, of course you're expected to send it back, but what do you do if you simply don't like the wine? Tradition says that you should send a wine back only if it has gone bad, but Americans are much newer to wine and the whole concept of wine service. Many restaurants show quite a bit of flexibility when it comes to rejecting a wine, even if the wine is not faulty, so go ahead and send it back if you like—it's really your option. If a wine is actually faulty, the restaurant won't lose a penny because they will get their money back from the wholesaler who sold it to them; that is the normal process of doing business in the wine trade. On the other hand, if there is nothing wrong with the bottle of the wine, the restaurant has the option of serving it by the glass to other patrons or simply offering it to another table. Don't feel pressured to drink a bottle of wine that you don't want with your meal.

Don't Stew

If you're unhappy with your service in a restaurant, speak up; don't sit and stew. Send the wine back, ask for a different table, and mention immediately that an item is too cold, too hot, or not what you ordered. It's called the "hospitality industry" for a reason.

The best way to avoid a bad experience at a restaurant is to avoid the problems early in the meal. Some restaurants will actually give you inferior tables because you're unrecognized—sort of that old French snobby thing! I will not take a bad table that is too near the kitchen, next to a strange column, or odd in some other way if it can be circumvented. Obviously, on a busy night like Saturday night, you may have to settle for a drafty table, but let the person seating you know upfront that you'd rather wait for a better seating location. The reason I'm so fussy about this is because it's the first impression of the meal and service, especially if it's a special occasion and you're a bit nervous; it sets the stage for the rest of the meal.

Once I was in a DC restaurant that was notorious for placing first-timers in their seating "Siberia" —a spot isolated and hidden from the rest of the diners, with cramped seating, no view, and not very nice at all. This is where a compliment to the host/hostess works wonders.

Yes, we live in a democracy, and all people should be treated equally, whether they are rich or poor, or know anything about dining, wine, or often have simply been seen in the restaurant in the past. But the reality is many restaurants have unwritten codes that regulars get better seating, service, and, frankly, a better meal. My strategy is simple: rarely does anyone say something positive to the host stand about the chef or the sommelier. I try to create the impression that I'm really looking forward to this meal, because I've heard such great things about the restaurant and their four-star chef, and I hear the sommelier is terrific. It's one of my old sales tactics; schmooze the people who rarely get treated very well, and it often works. I've received better tables, a free glass of wine from the sommelier (you're obligated at that point to purchase a bottle!), and sometimes a free extra course. Being genteel and honestly interested in what a restaurant has accomplished is what the hospitality industry is all about. If you walk in with a superior attitude and treat people beneath you (remember, I live in DC!) with condescension, you may get a cold response in return.

EXERCISE 10: Imagine you've just been hired by a very fancy fine dining restaurant to be their wine server/sommelier. For whatever reason, they forgot to check your background and you decide to at least try the job for one day with your current level of wine knowledge. You don't know anything about the wine list, so it's completely new to you. Your first customer requesting wine service at dinner is...you—actually you! How would you explain to this identical twin of yourself which wine to choose? Think about all the emotions, confusions, and contradictions in your mind—you don't have to worry about the customer's reaction, because it's you! Think about what you would say to yourself to be at ease and to lessen the tension of the situation...don't forget to take a few slow deep breaths so that you can return to a relaxed state. When you are finished with this exercise, you will be very comfortable and relaxed about choosing a wine. This is your "Restaurant Wine Experience."

Exercise 11: Imagine you're walking into a wine store that you recognize near your neighborhood. Think about the exterior displays and any other visual marketing items that you might see, probably a "sale" sign. Now visualize yourself opening the door of the store and seeing hundreds of different bottles of wine each stacked neatly in different aisles. You are going to confidently walk up through the first aisle you see, take fifteen steps and turn to your left and the perfect bottle of wine is waiting for you. Pick up the bottle and proceed directly to the store checkout. As you're walking to the checkout, think of the positive feelings you get all over your body, that feeling of accomplishment when you've just completed a relatively complicated task with ease. Revel in the moment, you can even smile a little, maybe have a giggle, you've just become an accomplished wine purchaser! This is your "Store Wine Experience."

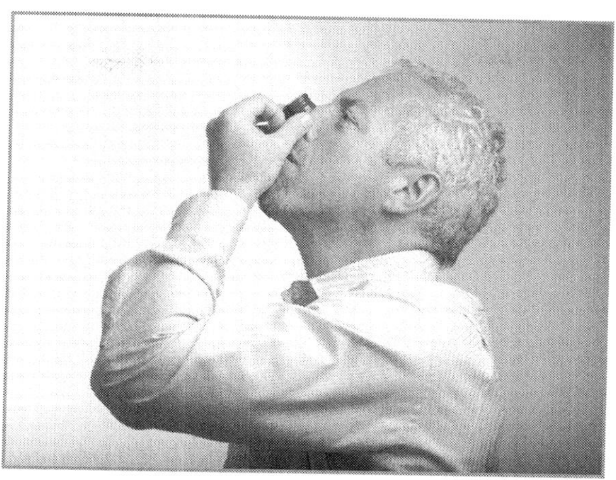

TASTING IS A SERIOUS BUSINESS!

9. LOOSE ENDS

You know that the more you explore the wine world, the more often you'll meet the know-it-alls and the pretentious. In my experience, these people are insecure and don't know what they're talking about pertaining to wine. Avoid them or escape as quickly as possible.

Noble rot is just another case where a mistake in nature opened up people's eyes to a better way.

Just Dessert

People always ask me about dessert wines. I guess it's human nature to have a sweet tooth. There is something enjoyable about a well-made dessert wine, and the key is to get the sweetness in balance with the wine's acidity, so that it won't be cloyingly sweet. You guessed it—this is the same as when you're cooking—seek to have the same balance in wine as there is in cuisine. If you remember the chemistry formula from chapter 3, no sugar is left over after the yeast eats the sugar and turns it into alcohol and CO_2. There are a few ways that sugar can be retained in the wine (and remember, we wine professionals call that the "residual sugar"). The grapes can have so much sugar remaining late in the harvest that the yeast can't eat it all, you can lower the temperature during fermentation so that the yeast stops fermenting, or you can add alcohol so that the yeast die and leave the sugar in the wine.

Some terms you'll hear around dessert wine include "late harvest," "noble rot," and "fortified wine."

Late Harvest

In cooler wine-growing regions, grapes often ripen so late in the season that the weather cools down in the fall and leaves plenty of sugar in the grapes as well as high acidity levels, due to the cool climate. Sometimes, there's so much sugar, that the yeast can't finish the fermentation job, and this leaves the sugars in the wine. Certain regions like in Germany, Austria, and Alsace, France, are known for these late harvest wines. (The French call them "Vendange Tardive," the Germans have the Auslese, Beerenauslese, and Trochenbeerenauslese.) You can get dessert wines from many regions, but the cooler regions retain the highest acidities that make these wines more balanced.

Noble Rot

The term "noble rot" comes from a mold called botrytis that actually attacks grapes and their sugars late in the ripening cycle. It can actually destroy grapes, but late in the season, it rots the grapes and increases the concentration of the sugars, making for an unbelievably unctuous sweet dessert wine. The world's most famous region for this is Sauternes in France, and the world's most expensive is D'Yquem, which can sell for hundreds of dollars a half-bottle (375ml). These wines, like late-harvest wines, retain their acidities to counterbalance the high sugars and keep the wine refreshing on your palate. The pairing for dessert wines can be desserts—remember 1+1=1/2—so sweet wine and sweet dessert seem less sweet, but I much prefer salty or even fatty. The traditional pairing is foie gras with Sauterne because a sweet wine with fatty goose or duck liver is a great combination.

When I was in Bordeaux, we often started the meal with an aperitif of Sauternes.

Sometimes, breaking the wine rules makes for a more pleasurable experience. Even though the wine rules say to go from sparkling to dry whites to reds and then onto dessert wines, serving in that order, starting with a dessert wine actually relaxes the digestion and offers something sweet with a nice acidity that gets your taste buds ready for dinner. If you think about it, many Americans start their meal with a cocktail, which is often sweetened in some way, so beginning with dessert wines is for the same reason. When you enjoy a nice meal in France, it's not unusual to have a before-dinner drink, wine with dinner, finishing with an after-dinner drink, sometimes called a "digestif." If you've never enjoyed a slow, leisurely, French-style, multicourse meal, I guarantee you it's worth the wait!

Fortified Wine

The story goes that, a few hundred years ago, when wine was shipped in the hulls of boats, the heat from travel would destroy the wine. Someone figured out that adding alcohol, normally brandy, to the wine, preserved it against spoilage and heat became its friend.

Yeast can actually be killed if it produces too much alcohol, but another way to stop yeast in action and leave residual sugar is to simply add alcohol to the point yeast dies, and this is called a "fortified wine." Many really cheap rotgut wines you see in stores are made this way, but some of the world's great dessert wines like port, Madeira, and sherry are as well. Alcohol not only kills the yeast, but it becomes an antibacterial preservative as well, and this is one of the reasons why fortified wines can age for decades. If you're into port, there are three main kinds: ruby, tawny, and vintage. Ruby is the traditional style aged in bottles. Tawny is actually "preaged" in oak casks, which means that oxygen has had time to slowly oxidize the wine and creates the caramel color associated with this style. Ruby tends to have fresher red fruit color and flavor; tawny is more caramelized. Most ports are produced "nonvintage," which means the juice comes from grapes of many different years' blends, but every few years in a decade, a great vintage occurs, and winemakers create a special one-year-only "vintage" port. These tend to be of a high quality but often cost much more.

Everyone seems to be curious about dessert wines, but they obviously aren't purchased that much, since they sit on retailers' shelves forever!

I think the reality of dessert wines is that they are fun for a half glass or full glass, but it's difficult for even two people to finish a half bottle due to the sugar content. Although they actually store pretty well once they're opened for maybe a week (I've left fortified ports out for a month, and they still are pretty fresh), it's mostly consumed as a special-occasion wine. The traditional pairing for port is blue cheese and walnuts. Blue cheese is very salty, so you have salty vs. sweet, and walnuts are actually tannic, and this counterbalances the sometimes-bitter tannin compounds of port. Cooking with dessert wines, especially port, is a great way to make a syrupy sweet reduction, which can work with meat but also works great as a dessert topping.

Thanksgiving Wines

The number one article on wine every year is the Thanksgiving edition. For some reason, people actually believe that it's possible to pair this mixed-up meal.

People seem to get very stressed out about choosing wines for probably one of the most family-oriented American meals every year, the Thanksgiving turkey. The first rule of food and wine pairing is to drink what you like, and this meal fits that maxim perfectly; it's essentially an impossible meal to pair with wine! Turkey itself is normally the main protein, and turkey is about as bland as chicken, so any wine will go with it. It's the cranberry sauce, yams, stuffing, mashed potatoes, and a series of other dishes that create the pairing challenge.

If Uncle Sally and Aunt Ted (the audience laughs) show up with their jug-wine tastes, why waste a good bottle of wine on them? Put on the table some big bottles of the kind of cheap stuff they love, and, hide under the table your bottle just for you!

Thanksgiving seems like just another opportunity for the dysfunctional family to show its true colors. Why not avoid the potential for conflict and let the die-hard Ripple/white Zinfandel lovers have their tipple of choice? No matter how hard you try to impress everyone with your new wine-matching skills, people are stuck on their drinking habits, particularly a slightly older generation, and the day is one to commune, not to convert. I love the wine writers' suggestions for "Gewurztraminer with its spicy flavors perfectly matching the minced pie, while a nice Chablis will do great with the stuffing." Baloney! You need a wine that's middle range or neutral, so sparkling wine always works, and it's a great way to set the tone of celebration. Again, it's ridiculous to spend too much money on Champagne; go with a Cava or Prosecco for $15/bottle or less. Rosé, slightly chilled, goes great with pretty much all foods, but one more wine fits the bill.

Go Nouveau

Every year on the third Thursday of November, French law decrees that the Beaujolais Nouveau can be released to the public.

Beaujolais Nouveau is produced in the Beaujolais region of southern Burgundy, and it's produced from 100 percent of the red grape of Gamay. Due to some fancy winemaking and technology, this wine is made fresh and ready to drink as soon as it's bottled. It's a very low tannin-light tasting red wine that goes great with a wide variety of flavors that fit Thanksgiving dishes well. The price is right too. It's usually around $10 a bottle, and it's readily available in every wine store the week of Thanksgiving. And, yes, you buy that year's vintage, so if you're eating in 2011, the vintage will be 2011. I'm not even sure it ages long enough to last an extra year, but it might be fun to try an older bottle!

Probably the high point of my winery visits was a special brunch with Jean Luc Thunevin and his lovely wife Muriel, after a tour of one of the highest rated wineries in Bordeaux in the world, Chateaux Ausone. We ate delicious eggs with truffles and tenderloin of beef all paired with Valandraud and Ausone's wines in their quaint little dining room above the world's most famous "garage" wine-making facility. You just can't recreate moments like that!

Visiting Wineries

Ever since the movie *Sideways*, visiting wineries has been a great weekend escape or now a great way to spend the majority of your vacation in destinations like Napa Valley, California; Williamette, Oregon; or Tuscany, Italy. The United States is a bit different than Europe in that wineries here cater to the general public and often have tasting rooms, set tours, and other entertainment, while in Europe this is a newer phenomenon. In my backyard in Virginia, on any weekend there are many events such as music festivals, wine tastings, wine tours, wine pairings, weddings, and a whole gamut of activities to get people to spend their money in wine country. The most obvious reason that wineries hold public activities in the United States is to increase high-margin wine sales. In the United States, most states and jurisdictions have the three-tier system, which means that a winery must sell to a wholesaler who, in turn, sells to a retailer that ends up selling to you, the consumer. For example, if you pay $18 for a bottle of wine, the winemaker may get only $7 or $8 of that; the rest goes to the two other intermediaries. If you go to a winery and purchase wine directly, the winery gets all of that $18, which increases their profit margin but also gives them the incentive to invite visitors. Thus is the creation of wine tourism, a whole new growth industry in the United States and potentially a new avenue for creative businesses that find ways to help both Americans and international tourists visit, experience, and explore our wine country.

I love to travel for wine and food and meet people who produce great artisanal products from cheese and wine to olive oil. Vineyards are always fun, but experiencing a multicourse meal in the wine cellar is even more fantastic!

Wine and Travel

I've been on many wine and food tours throughout the world, both professionally and as a casual consumer. Some of the high points for me include the Vinitaly wine conference in Verona, Italy, where four thousand wineries tasted their wines; the Bordeaux tour, where we had private appointments with many elite wineries; the International Pinot Noir Conference in McMinnville, Oregon, where in just over two and a half days, I must have tasted well over a hundred Pinot Noirs; and the Charleston Food and Wine Festival, where I had the best food of any festival I've ever been to—well, maybe the New Orleans Food and Wine Festival had pretty good food too!

Many people come up to me after class and ask if I have any advice when they choose a certain wine destination. My normal reply is to go to the Internet and choose a place to stay that is near the wineries, so that the drive is short and you can experience more wineries. If all I'm doing is visiting wineries in a day, I can normally visit about four: two in the morning and two in the afternoon. If you want to maximize winery visits, it's smart to pack a quick lunch, like sandwiches, but it's also great fun to enjoy a seated wine lunch or wine dinner where the courses and wine are laid out for you. Things to consider include being chauffeured around or driving yourself, or even if you want to go on a wine tour. I've been on many wine tours, because I hate planning travel and I get the added benefit of better tours, being with people who love wine, and the chance to have private meetings with the winemakers. Some tours include all meals, while others don't, so this has a big effect on the price. There are even unique tours, now, where you can hike in the vineyards, travel by bike throughout Europe, and go on the barge tours of France. There are many options, but as the price tag gets higher, you can also expect the attendees to be older as well.

Make a Small Fortune

The one truism you'll always hear from wine professionals is, "Do you know how to make a small fortune? Invest a large fortune in the wine industry."

Ask any European or American vintners, for that matter, and they'll tell you that it's very difficult to break even, much less make a profit producing wine. The simple reason is that, unlike other agricultural endeavors, where you simply plant crops, vines take a few years before they even produce quality grapes for wine making, and many things stop the grapes from completely ripening. This, plus the fact that you have to invest in equipment to produce the wine, including a winemaker and barrels to store the wine, are all reasons the endeavor is expensive and time consuming. Economics determines what you can charge for your wine and also what you'll have to pay for grapes if you purchase them. If you don't have the passion for wine, don't get into the business. There are better financial payoffs elsewhere.

Storing Wine

You don't need a fancy cellar or expensive wine cellar storage system to store your wine; just find a place that's relatively dark, cool, and free of vibration.

When I bought a new house in 2003, I thought I might want to turn part of my basement into a wine cellar with all the bells and whistles: humidity and temperature controls, redwood racks, lots of designer motifs, and even a special wine door with etched glass. When the bill came back for a two-thousand-bottle wine cellar at over $20,000, I realized that my $99 metal wire wine racks had served me well (They hold 144 bottles each. I still have them!). I did quite a bit of research, but came up with a very simple formula for wine storage: if you have a cool place that's relatively dark and doesn't have too much vibration, you can store your wine there. It's best to store wines on their sides if they have cork closures (cork can dry out otherwise and allow air into your wine), but other than that, everything else is pretty optional, even wine racks. There are some fancy wine refrigerators now available that are affordable and, if you entertain at all, they are nice to have, but they're really designed to keep your wines at the proper serving temperature, not necessarily for long-term storage. If you have wines that are especially valuable to you or they're rare, then you might want to consider professional wine storage, which is available in many cities. Expect to pay around $18 to $50 for a twelve-bottle case per year, so it really only makes sense for wines that have some value to you.

INVESTING IN WINE CAN BE VERY PROFITABLE – IN THE WORST CASE SCENARIO, YOU CAN ALWAYS DRINK YOUR LOSSES!

Investing in Wine

You can make money investing in wine, but it involves some planning, understanding, and logistics. For example, where and how you store the wine makes a huge difference in the wines' final value. If things don't work out, on the other hand, you can always drink your losses!

When I first caught the wine bug, I only wanted to hold and store wines for drinking purposes. I would age some in my cellar on racks for maybe five or ten years when they were ready to drink, but my sole purpose of collecting was to imbibe. At some point, after hearing about pretty aggressive returns on investing in wine, and after having a serious talk about how to invest and make decent returns in wine from a local retailer, I decided to give it a try. I bought some investment-grade wines from the retailer from the Bordeaux 2000 vintage which Robert Parker had also scored as perfect one hundred points. These wines have created solid returns for me, but it is a very specialty investment: you have to buy them, store them professionally and, ultimately, sell them. Each process is work!

Definition "wine futures": Wine Futures (also known as "En Primeur") refers to buying wine after it is made and put into barrels, but before it is bottled. Samples are taken from the casks, and wine reviewers score the wine over a period of years, so that purchasers can predict the quality of the final wine. The wine is generally bottled and shipped around two years later.

If you're serious about investing in wine, whether to make money or simply to pay for your other wine purchases (this is a British tradition), then treat it like any investment. Do your research. Bordeaux and Burgundy are the benchmarks for investment-grade wines, and with a few other exceptions, they are what you want to bet your money on. You need to purchase the top producers in the best vintages, with the best wine-critic scores, and you have to store them properly and just wait. Another value factor is that, generally, the larger the bottle of wine, the more value—in other words a magnum, which is double the size of a standard wine bottle, is often worth well more than double the value of a bottle half its size. If you want the best returns, then you should buy wines as "futures," which means the grapes have been harvested and fermented into barrels, but before they are actually bottled and shipped. There are many risks to doing this, including the way critics score the wine each year, but there are also commensurate higher returns. Again, this is a very risky venture—be prepared to drink your losses!

Big Bucks

Going back to the value equation in wine, when you purchase wine as an investment, you can expect to pay very high relative prices for the wine. A top Bordeaux wine can easily cost over $500 for a standard-size bottle, and they can also be purchased in larger formats like magnums (1.5 liters), double magnums (3 liters), and Impériales (6 liters). The reason these wines have such incredibly high value is that there are, surprisingly, many multimillionaires throughout the world who can afford such luxuries. If someone can afford four homes, a private jet, and a yacht, then a $1,500 bottle of Chateau Latour 2005 isn't such an extravagance. These kind of wine prices are set by supply and demand; recent studies have actually shown that the top investment-grade wine prices are directly related to the number of billionaires in the world today!

EXERCISE 12: Think back to a moment when you were at a celebration and wine was involved: a wedding, victory dinner, or maybe a reception around the holidays—opening a bottle of Champagne or another sparkling wine works well to jog your memory! Close your eyes and think about the excitement in the air, the revelry and the overall good cheer. Get all your senses involved with the moment including the smiles on people's faces, sounds of laughter and cheer, and the positive emotional feelings of everyone involved. Now imagine the popping sound of an exploding Champagne cork. Keep listening to the popping sound over and over again for a few minutes until it is set in your mind. Simply associate the sound of the Champagne cork popping with the celebration's experiences. This is your "Wine Celebration Experience."

Don't Take Wine Too Seriously!

10. CONCLUSION: I DRINK, THEREFORE I AM

Charlie is attending a free wine tasting held at a local liquor store.

Attendee: "You seem to know a lot about wine. How did you learn so much?"

Charlie: "I'm in the business. I'm a full-time wine professional. I run TasteDC."

Attendee: "So what's your favorite wine?"

Charlie: "RED!"

Attendee: "Are Virginia wines any good?"

Charlie: "If you mean all the wines from Virginia, or for that matter from any region in the world, including my favorite regions in France and Italy, the answer would be no. But each wine region produces wines that are unique and special to that locality. You have to seek out the best of each region and avoid copycats!

Charlie: "Thank you, everyone, for coming and, if I can leave you one last thought: a meal without wine is breakfast—good night!" The audience applauds and a few people who especially enjoyed the class or who have a serious burning question come up to Charlie at the end. Most of the time, people just want to thank Charlie and mention that they're going to Napa Valley soon or some other destination. Maybe Charlie has some recommendations. End-of-the-evening questions tend to have a personal connection to the questioner—maybe they also had an embarrassing experience with a corked wine at a restaurant, or a really difficult moment at a wine tasting. Charlie continues to drink his last glass of wine, which is normally the red Bordeaux that reminds him that this is not such a bad job after all: no desk, no boss, and his office is in front of the crowd entertaining people who are on their way to new wine experiences.

After Charlie answers the last person's question, it's time to go home. Charlie is physically and emotionally spent, but he has that sense of satisfaction that keynote speakers or comedians often get after a show. He feels a bit sore and tired but, at the same time, exhilarated. He thanks the volunteers who have mostly left already at this point, packs up unopened bottles of wine, and takes a half-full bottle with him, surreptitiously hidden in the box with the rest. He's thinking this bottle will taste delicious when he gets home and lounges on the couch with his feet up on the coffee table with his favorite *Kung Fu* show on TV. Life is good. Sleep will come soon.

Enjoying wine is more about the journey than the final destination. I've included a list of the exercises that ended each chapter at the end of this book in the appendix. These exercises will help you better focus on different situations you'll be dealing with in the future with wine. They are all "experiences," which means that they relate to the right side of your brain. You can use them for specific situations when you need help. Say for example, you're in a restaurant and you're nervous about ordering wine. Go back to Exercise 10, "Restaurant Wine Experience," and explore your thoughts and feelings again. Possibly, you're very new to wine and you want to increase your confidence, so you decide to invite some people over for hors d'oeuvres and wine. Go back to Exercise 1, "Original Wine Experience," and Exercise

12, "Wine Celebration Experience," to reinforce yourself and feel confidence in your decision. Remember: you never stop learning; certainly, we all have more to see and taste!

Topics you may want to pursue further include learning more about various wine regions and types of wine and labels. I didn't feel this book should cover that, because wine rules constantly change, and rules that were written in stone no longer apply. The French, who so revere their strict regulations on AOC wines, are currently changing them to fit the times; expect to see more French wines that are varietally labeled. Just as New World winemakers are comfortable using technology to make their wine taste the way a chemist would choose, they're going back to "natural" wine making and learning the ways of sustainability and how to better let nature take its course to make beautiful wines. There is always the dichotomy of wine, the nature vs. nurture conflict. Is it worth paying more money for what nature gives you or is it better to find a cheaper alternative through the use of modern science? To put the question into perspective for you, ask yourself if you would be willing to pay $6 a pint for locally grown blueberries when you can get, say, a Chilean variety for $3 a pint. As you progress with wine, your tastes will change.

And that's the key to understanding what *Wine Basics 101* is all about and what I've spent the last twelve years attempting to do: introduce one perspective on eating and drinking, that wine should simply go with the meal. I've been looked down upon and told that I'm wrong about wine, that there are nuances that take decades if not a lifetime to understand, secret societies that know the true meaning of "in vino veritas," wine and food combinations that only someone who is trained as a chef or sommelier can understand. I'm telling you, I've met many of these alleged experts, and frankly, many of them don't know what they're talking about. If I tell you that a wine is good and I show you my credentials, and you take my word for it, would you also listen to me if I told you that the steak you've been enjoying for many years is no good or that your choice of shoes is all wrong? You have to ultimately learn what you like, and all I can do at TasteDC is give you the opportunity. Now it's your job to use your senses to learn.

Eating well and drinking well go together. If you're willing to invest in a better steak, an artisanal piece of cheese, or an organic apple, it's worth it to learn a little bit about wine. Before you know it, you'll be choosing wine like a pro!

Conclusion—bringing this whole class together, you have tasted a variety of "styles" of wine. You now have some basic wine language and lingo. You have a list of wine types you either like or don't. And now you know how your choice of food plays into the wine equation. Now it's up to you to explore the world of wine.

So what is it that I love so much about my job that I'd like to do this for the rest of my life? I love that I've chosen an industry that is still young and developing and that I can put my personal mark on the wine world. I will never know everything about wine, but that has never been my intent. I enjoy learning and exploring new facts about wine as well as tasting unique food and wine combinations and meeting so many different kinds of people getting into the business. I want to explore new food products, taste the great dishes of the world, and wash it all down with wine, craft beers, single malt whiskies, and maybe a sake or two. I want to share these experiences with others who love wine and food, and I want to be a part of a growing lifestyle where people feel comfortable breaking bread together from all walks of life. It's just as exciting for me to share a meal with a farmer and his family in a little village, as it is to sit for five hours or so and have a twelve-course wine dinner with over twenty wines.

Just remember, if you see me out anywhere, from a wine festival to out in the vineyard and I've had a little too much to taste...I'm Charlie Adler, and I drink on the job.

Appendix: Wine Exercises

Exercise 1: Think about your first pleasant experience with wine—this should preferably be a memory from when you were younger. Close your eyes and take a few minutes to imagine the people around you at the time, the wine itself, its container, and any sounds, sights, or smells you associate with the mental picture. Try to picture what type of event was occurring: a celebration, a special occasion, or any other details about the moment. Did you taste the wine or did you simply watch others enjoy it? Think about how you felt in general and your first associations with the experience. Try to make it vivid in your mind by accentuating the images, sounds, and smells. This is your "Original Wine Experience."

Exercise 2: Think about a recent experience when you shared wine with a friend or friends—this should preferably be a memory within the last few months or weeks. Just as in Exercise 1, close your eyes and take a few minutes to imagine the people around you at the time, the wine itself, its container, and any sounds, sights, or smells you associate with the mental picture. This time, try to really concentrate on the wine or wines you were drinking at the time and on any foods you were eating as part of the moment. Really try to imagine the scene and the people: and anything that was said that made you laugh or think about the moment. Can you taste the wine and food right now in your mind? Try to make it vivid in your mind by accentuating the images, sounds, and smells. This is your "Now Wine Experience."

Exercise 3: Close your eyes, and imagine yourself sitting in front of a wine glass on a table. Think about its shape, type of glass or crystal, the stem, the rim, and how the light shines on it. Now imagine a bottle of red wine next to it that is already open. Pick up the bottle of wine and pour a good amount into the glass, fill it up about a third of the way up the glass. Now take your hand and hold it carefully at the glass's stem and swirl the wine on the table so that you can "see" the wine rotating around the glass in a soft wave. Now pick up the glass, look at the wine again and bring the glass right up to your nose and sniff—it helps at this point if you actually "sniff" through your nose, even though this is just an imaginary exercise. Now put the glass back down and think about the aromas—consider the type of fruit, maybe cherries, then think a bit about the spiciness or earthiness of the wine. Since you may be new to the aromas of wine, think of a smell you would recognize in a room, say cherry or cinnamon apple pie—it doesn't matter if this is how the win really smells, it's just the fact that you're having a sensory perception. Now pick up the glass of wine and bring it to your lips and take a sip—imagine the wine touching your tongue and giving you a pleasant taste, maybe you get a very cherry flavor or you can feel the smooth texture of the wine. Spend a few moments just appreciating the wine on your tongue and the lovely aromas in the nose of the wine. Now, put the glass back down on the table and relax for a minute or so and enjoy the pleasure throughout your body and senses. This is the "Tasting Moment"—you will think about this the next few times you sample a glass of wine.

Exercise 4: Take a seat and imagine in front of you a small strawberry plant—it doesn't need to be accurate, just imagine some green leaves and a small plant. Watch the leaves grow and flowers begin to appear as the plant begins to get bushier. Soon white flowers will appear and you will see little immature green fruit begin to appear. Slowly watch as the green fruit gets larger and larger and then redder and redder until the fruit begins to swell with juice and color. Imagine picking a green early fruit and biting into it. The flavor will be bitter and sour with little sugar and make you pucker. Pick another riper strawberry and taste how the sour becomes sugary sweet. Pick an extra ripe grape that is really red and bursting with flavor and taste the incredible sweetness—notice that the sour flavor is gone. This is your "Ripe Fruit Experience."

Exercise 5: Imagine yourself walking through a vineyard. If you've visited vineyards in the past, use any visual imagery in your mind, otherwise, just imagine walking down the rows and rows of vines. As you walk, think about the sounds of nature like birds singing and crickets chirping. Feel the sun warming your body and giving you positive sensations. Now you'll see a large bunch of red grapes: pick an especially ripe red grape from the vine and pop it into your mouth. Feel the sweet and sour sensation of the juice, even let a little squirt out onto your shirt; it's OK, you're in wine country! Feel the slight crunch of the seeds on your teeth, but spit them out before they get too bitter. Take another grape and more carefully bite through the skin being careful not to crush the seeds at all. This time feel the rough texture of the skin on your tongue, even roll it around a bit and get the sensations. Let the sweet, sour, and bitter sensations languish on your tongue and senses for a few moments. This is your "Wine Grape Sensation."

Exercise 6: This time you are going to do a simple physical experiment. Go out and purchase some tea bags of preferably a black or dark tea and a small container of heavy cream. Get two tea cups/mugs and put a single tea bag in one cup and two tea bags in the other tea cup. Add almost boiling water in each cup, let steep in the one-tea-bag cup for about three minutes and a few minutes longer for the two-bag cup before removing both tea bags. First taste the single-tea-bag cup of tea and get a sense for the astringency and rough texture on your tongue. Drink a little water and take about a one minute break, and then taste the two-tea-bag tea and get a sense of the same roughness and texture on your tongue. Put about one or two teaspoons of cream in each tea cup and stir thoroughly into the teas and taste the two teas again. You should notice that the cream "softens" the astringency—the same chemical tannins that give red wine astringency. Just as in tea, fat softens the red tannins in wine. This is your "Tannin Sensation."

Exercise 7: Seat yourself comfortably. Close your eyes and think back to a favorite moment of a trip you took far away from where you currently live. Think about a very pleasant experience you were having while dining and possibly the wine you were drinking at the time. Think about the newness of the experience, possibly people spoke a foreign language you didn't understand. Try to imagine the surroundings in your physical environment such as the plants, people, music, and aromatic smells. Think about how delicious the food and wine were and how you experienced something new for the first time. Accentuate in your mind the features you liked the most and make them larger than life. If there were any people involved, maybe you remember something entertaining about them, accentuate this trait and remember it. This is your "Positive Foreign Wine and Food Experience."

Exercise 8: Think about a food that you really crave occasionally, something that gets your taste buds excited and your stomach gurgling from hunger. Close your eyes and really look at the food item. Imagine how delicious it will taste when you put the first bite in your mouth, really think about the food, but hold back on the first bite. You want to get yourself salivating now, so think about what makes the food so irresistible. Maybe it's creamy and sweet or crunchy and salty, maybe it has a truly magnificent aroma, think deeply about it. Can you detect spices or seasonings, things like pepper, vanilla, fried oil, saltiness, etc.? Now take a big scoop of the food and slowly place it in your mouth and get all the sensations around your tongue and cheeks. Sense the temperature of the food, the texture, and how it coats your tongue or if it has roughness, if you have to chew it, think about how the different flavors come together after each chew. This is your "Memorable Food Sensation."

Exercise 9: As an experiment, you are going to experience 1+1=1/2. Find something sweet like a dried cherry or a piece of chocolate, and bite into it while drinking something sweet with it like juice or another sweetened drink. Notice your perception of sweetness in your mouth, does it increase or decrease? Try the same with two foods high in acidity, say green olives and Italian salad dressing. Bitter/tannic is a bit trickier, but you could try dark chocolate and black tea. Notice the change of sensations on your palate and how similar flavors seem to cancel each other out and bring out other flavors. Make a mental note of your experience. This is your "Food and Wine Pairing Experience."

Exercise 10: Imagine you've just been hired by a very fancy fine dining restaurant to be their wine server/sommelier. For whatever reason, they forgot to check your background and you decide to at least try the job for one day with your current level of wine knowledge. You don't know anything about the wine list, so it's completely new to you. Your first customer requesting wine service at dinner is..you—actually you! How would you explain to this identical twin of yourself which wine to choose? Think about all the emotions, confusions and contradictions in your mind—you don't have to worry about the customer's reaction, because it's you! Think about what you would say to yourself to be at ease and to lessen the tension of the situation..don't forget to take a few slow deep breaths so that you can return to a relaxed state. When you are finished with this exercise, you will be very comfortable and relaxed about choosing a wine. This is your "Restaurant Wine Experience."

Exercise 11: Imagine you're walking into a wine store that you recognize near your neighborhood. Think about the exterior displays and any other visual marketing items that you might see, probably a "sale" sign. Now visualize yourself opening the door of the store and seeing hundreds of different bottles of wine each stacked neatly in different aisles. You are going to confidently walk up through the first aisle you see, take fifteen steps and turn to your left and the perfect bottle of wine is waiting for you. Pick up the bottle and proceed directly to the store checkout. As you're walking to the checkout, think of the positive feelings you get all over your body, that feeling of accomplishment when you've just completed a relatively complicated task with ease. Revel in the moment, you can even smile a little, maybe have a giggle, you've just become an accomplished wine purchaser! This is your "Store Wine Experience."

Exercise 12: Think back to a moment when you were at a celebration and wine was involved: a wedding, victory dinner, or maybe a reception around the holidays—opening a bottle of Champagne or another sparkling wine works well to jog your memory! Close your eyes and think about the excitement in the air, the revelry and the overall good cheer. Get all your senses involved with the moment including the smiles on people's faces, sounds of laughter and cheer, and the positive emotional feelings of everyone involved. Now imagine the popping sound of an exploding Champagne cork. Keep listening to the popping sound over and over again for a few minutes until it is set in your mind. Simply associate the sound of the Champagne cork popping with the celebration's experiences. This is your "Wine Celebration Experience."

SELECT BIBLIOGRAPHY

Arnold, Eric. *First Big Crush: The Down and Dirty on Making Great Wine Down Under*. New York: Scribner, 2007.

Wine for the Confused. Director David Kennard. Koch Vision, 2004. DVD.

Colman, Tyler. *Wine Politics: How Governments, Environmentalists, Mobsters, and Critics Influence the Wines We Drink*. Berkeley: University of California Press, 2008.

Cox, Jeff. From *Vines to Wines: The Complete Guide to Growing Grapes and Making Your Own Wine*. North Adams: Storey Communications, U.S., 1999.

Echikson, William. *Noble Rot: A Bordeaux Wine Revolution*. New York: W. W. Norton & Company, 2004.

Esposito, Sergio. *Passion on the Vine: A Memoir of Food, Wine, and Family in the Heart of Italy*. New York: Broadway Books, 2008.

Feiring, Alice. *The Battle for Wine and Love: or How I Saved the World from Parkerization*. New York: Mariner Books, 2008.

Kamp, David. *The United States of Arugula: How We Became a Gourmet Nation*. New York: Broadway Books, 2006.

McCalman, Max and David Gibbons. *Cheese: A Connoisseur's Guide to the World's Best*. New York: Clarkson Potter, 2005.

Mccoy, Elin. *The Emperor of Wine: The Rise of Robert M. Parker, Jr. and the Reign of American Taste*. New York: Ecco Publishing, 2005.

Mondovino. Jonathan Nossiter. Studio: Velocity, 2005. DVD.

Sideways. Alexander Payne. 20th Century Fox, 2005. DVD

Pollan, Michael. *The Omnivore's Dilemma: A Natural History of Four Meals*. New York: Penguin Press, 2007.

Robinson, Jancis. *How to Taste: a Guide to Enjoying Wine,* New York: Simon & Schuster, 2008.

Rosenthal, Neal I. *Reflections of a Wine Merchant*. New York: Farrar, Straus and Giroux, 2008.

Big Night. Campbell Scott. Sony Pictures, 1998. DVD.

Siler, Julia Flynn. *The House of Mondavi: The Rise and Fall of an American Wine Dynasty*. New York: Gotham Books, 2007.

Smith , Andrew F. *The Oxford Companion to American Food and Drink*. New York: Oxford University Press, 2007.

Sokolin, David, and Alexandra Bruce. *Investing in Liquid Assets: Uncorking Profits in Today's Global Wine Market*. New York: Simon & Schuster, 2008.

Taber, George M. *Judgment of Paris: California vs. France and the Historic 1976 Paris Tasting That Revolutionized Wine*. New YorK: Scribner, 2005.

Taber, George M. *To Cork or Not To Cork: Tradition, Romance, Science, and the Battle for the Wine Bottle*. New York: Scribner, 2007.

Thomas, Tara Q. *The Complete Idiot's Guide to Wine Basics*. New York: Alpha, 2008.

Waters, Alice. *The Art of Simple Food: Notes, Lessons, and Recipes from a Delicious Revolution*. New York: Clarkson Potter, 2007.

Suggested Web Resources:

http://tv.winelibrary.com – Gary Vaynerchuk – the man, the legend, he is the ultimate king of wine!

www.localwineevents.com – The best resource on the Web for wine and food events

www.erobertparker.com – The nine-hundred-pound gorilla of wine critics, for $99 a year you get great reviews and scores

www.vinfolio.com – Great for buying or selling wine, also has excellent software for managing your wine inventory and valuing it

www.liv-ex.com –The Fine Wine Exchange, excellent for valuing high-end fine wines www.wine-searcher.com – excellent resource for locating wine, the Pro Version for an additional $29.95/year has even more great features

www.winezap.com – excellent resource for locating wine

www.decanter.com – British publication, subscribe to their free e-mail update service and receive international wine information

www.winespectator.com – both online and a magazine publication, great coverage of the wine world and industry for consumers

www.cellartracker.com – great way for you to keep inventory of your wine and share wine reviews

www.wine-lovers-page.com – great resource for wine appreciation

www.wineenthusiast.com – great resource for wine storage systems and accessories

www.wineappreciation.com – great resource for publications, wine storage systems, and accessories

INDEX

Mozzarella di Bufala Campana, 157.

Made in the USA
Charleston, SC
06 April 2010